FOOTY
THE GREAT LEVELLER

Copyright © 2023 Laurie Aghan and Nick Armistead

All rights reserved. No part of this publication may be reproduced, distributed, or transmitted in any form or by any means, including photocopying, recording, or other electronic or mechanical methods, without the prior written permission of the publisher, except in the case of brief quotations embodied in critical reviews and certain other noncommercial uses permitted by copyright law.

(*) greenhill

https://greenhillpublishing.com.au/

Aghan, Laurie (author)
Armistead, Nick (author)
Footy The Great Leveller: Celebrating Laurie Aghan's life in Aussie Rules
ISBN 978-1-923088-66-5
Biography

Typeset Calluna 10/14
Cover Image by Laurie Aghan
Cover and book design by Green Hill Publishing

Celebrating Laurie Aghan's
life in Aussie Rules

FOOTY
THE GREAT LEVELLER

LAURIE AGHAN and
NICK ARMISTEAD

FOREWORD

I am most pleased to pen these few words about my staunch mate, Laurie Aghan, who overcame extreme difficulties in his early years to achieve great success throughout his life.

Growing up in Port Melbourne and South Melbourne was never easy as he had to withstand the gibes about his skin colour and his lack of so-called culture. But Laurie had plenty of intestinal fortitude which he put to good use in his sporting endeavours, specifically boxing and football.

He always possessed inner confidence to succeed in whatever he took on. This he achieved in spades; be it sport or business.

Laurie earned the admiration of many in his early years which has continued to this day. He has lived an amazing life and has conquered all that has been thrown at him.

In saying that, his wife Lorna has been his rock. His children, Kimberly and Jason, they've always received the love that he desperately missed.

I am proud to say that Laurie is a special friend and I thank him for this opportunity to write these few words. They feel somewhat inadequate in the big picture, but it is a great honour to speak about my great mate.

JOHN MAY

I first met Laurie in 1983 when he was invited to apply for the Melbourne Football Club's Reserve Coaching position. Unaware of his extensive and successful coaching background, my first impression was that he was undoubtedly a passionate and devoted football person. When quizzed on his coaching policies, tactics, and strategies I was not totally convinced that he had the acumen to be a successful coach at VFL Reserve Grade level.

Some years later, through football and a mutual friend, our paths crossed again, and a close and long-standing friendship evolved. I was reminded by Laurie, early in the reunion, that he thought that I was a little pompous at the interview and that I was the 'prick' who prevented him from having a successful VFL coaching career – a story he still relays when introducing me to any new associate.

It was through Laurie that I was introduced and accepted into his close group of childhood mates, commonly and appropriately known as 'The Portites'. It was through this group that I learned of Laurie's remarkable childhood struggles and survival experiences, and his dogged and determined drive to succeed both in sport and business – in many cases against the odds.

Our intense shared interest in sport was always going to glue our relationship. Despite our opposing loyalties to the Carlton and Melbourne Football Clubs, mutual respect was/is always evident when our clubs meet. Twenty plus years playing golf together has been an unforgettable experience – serious & competitive, yet mostly hilarious.

Owning and operating a successful business, numerous European jaunts taking in the exotic Italian Amalfi Coast, the Greek Islands, and a magical Alaskan cruise, along with his outstanding football coaching records culminating in his Old

Scotch 'Coach of the Century' nomination, were perhaps childhood pie-in-the-sky dreams achieved by Laurie and a measure of his life successes from his humble beginning.

As the years pass, I often reflect, and question DID I actually prevent Laurie from having a Victorian Football League coaching career – a life goal that he would have loved and cherished?

I'm sure you can make your own mind up after reading this recollection of Laurie's incredible life.

HASSA MANN

1

THE BEGINNING

> 'The measure of who we are is how we react to
> something that doesn't go our way.'
> **GREG POPOVICH, SAN ANTONIO SPURS.**

A WEEK BEFORE MY mother passed, I received a phone call from her husband - not my father, believe me - asking if I would visit her as she only had days left to live.

Can you just do it for her, Lawrence?

I hardly even know her mate. I wouldn't know what to say.

That's fine. I'm sure she'd just love to see you.

Fuck, OK.

I was the eldest of eight children – Len, Valda, Dorothy, Joy, Athol, Robert, and Jimmy Arthur – each of whom inherited our names from either our parents, uncles, or aunts. As a family who embraced the traditional system of naming children after their elders, that's certainly where the familial sentiment ended.

We were always fragmented. Like a team without a coach, there was no leadership in our family. We never received parental love and to be perfectly honest, we should not have even eventuated.

My mother, Irene Newman, came from a large family in Port Melbourne. Without wanting to sound crude or bad mouth her in any way, she could reasonably be described as a strange woman and a bit dippy. I can't remember a time when she showed any positive emotion towards us kids. In fact, as an adult I only saw her twice: once when our daughter Kimberley was born and the other while on her deathbed in St Kilda East.

There was a lot of apprehension that day followed by a lot of apologies and even more tears. She wasn't a good mother, but I also wasn't going to allow her to die believing I hated her. At that point, I guess I didn't.

Growing up in South Melbourne, my father Lawrence learnt to work hard and, like many of his era, show little emotion. His work as a stable hand meant he started at 4am seven days a week, breaking in horses and mucking out stables. He was regarded as one of the best horsemen in the area. He drove a double horse cart in those days and allowed me to tag along. While he would shovel up all the horse shit into a large brick enclosure, I would help him by raking over the straw with an old iron rake. I was only a young bloke and of little assistance, but I felt as though he appreciated the company.

Like Mum, my father's ability to show any affection to us kids was non-existent. He saved that for his mates. They often said he was one of the best street fighters they'd seen. He was loyal, staunch, and would offer them his unwavering support in any situation. I never saw that in him. Throughout the early years,

FOOTY THE GREAT LEVELLER

I remember him as a heavy drinker who didn't mind handing out the occasional flogging. Of course, as the eldest, I copped most of the beatdowns because I was 'the instigator'. It also helped him rationalise his actions because I was the most capable of taking a hit. This only ever happened when he was pissed out of his mind, forcing me to escape his wrath by climbing onto the roof of our two-story house.

He wasn't like that all the time. When I was playing for the Montague Rovers in the Sunday League, a teammate of mine, Squeaker Parkinson, once told me my father had been coming to watch me play footy for the past six weeks.

Are you kidding me?

Not at all Abbsy, he's been coming with me dad and watching from the car. So, you might want to try and get a kick next week.

Even when I was playing in the VFA a few years later, he would attend my games but never once told me he was there.

This unspoken interest in me was a common theme when it came to my father. Former Port Melbourne FC General Manager, Barry Kidd, used to drink with Laurie Sr. and said he would constantly discuss me and my footy like he was the host of his own sports show. Fuck, he never told me.

When my mother and father married in 1936 - much to the chagrin of the Newman's - Irene gave birth to me less than a year later. They were never suited for one another, but it didn't stop them from producing another seven children throughout their turbulent on-again/off-again relationship.

Despite my father's work ethic, the sheer number of mouths to feed meant we were facing financial hurdles at every turn. We were suffering from extreme poverty and, it is for this reason, we moved in with our paternal grandparents at 213 Coventry Street in South Melbourne.

It was a double-story timber home with a small lounge, an even smaller kitchen and six bedrooms. It boasted one outside toilet in a tiny shed, and a bathroom with a chip heater and a galvanised tub that we'd bathe in once a week.

While the idea of six bedrooms gives the allusion of space and privacy, the fact is we weren't the only ones living there. A number of aunts and uncles were in a similar financial position to my parents and, as such, there were 14 staying under the one roof.

The living conditions were awful. We slept six in a bed with a three-by-three top and tail set-up, while the lack of maintenance left the house in a constant state of ill repair with wallpaper hanging off the walls in each room.

The worst aspect of the overcrowded Coventry Street co-op was the constant fighting and arguing between the adults. Many nasty incidents occurred at the house and, given the close proximity of the residents, us kids were always exposed to it. After too many drinks, there were often heated arguments that resulted in punch-ups between my father and his brothers. There were affairs taking place under our roof, with one uncle sleeping with his brother's wife while he was at work. As kids, we saw it and we heard it. It was disgusting behaviour, and it played a major role in forming a deep-seated hatred for most of my family while growing up.

Family meals were extremely basic; stews, sausages, chops, and saveloys – the cheaper and nastier the better. At one stage, 12 cartons of camp pie fell off the back of a truck out the front of our house which resulted in the world's worst compressed meat and jelly being served up almost every day of the week for two years.

On special occasions, like Friday nights when the adults were half cut, we would buy fish and chips. They were profitable nights for me. The two or three of us kids who were sent to purchase the take-away would always hope to receive sixpence each. We'd then use only a portion of the money to buy the chips or potato cakes and pocket the remainder. If there's one lesson we could take from our underprivileged childhood, it was the value of money.

One traditional meal that was a constant throughout childhood was the Sunday Roast. Unfortunately, us kids would be resigned to the vegetarian lifestyle because there was never any meat left once the adults had served themselves. It certainly didn't help our quest for a succulent roast pork when Nan would regularly invite strays in for a feed if they were struggling. Not only did my grandparents provide shelter for the 12 of us, but they also looked after the local derelicts. That's just the way they were. Perhaps this is of little surprise when one considers they produced 11 children of their own.

Every Christmas or birthday, us kids received a hand-carved wooden toy from Nan and Pop. Meaningful enough but never a threat of being stolen by the local ratpack. Unfortunately, this didn't account for the blue pedal car my parents gave me one Christmas. It was easily the best present I ever received and one that I owned for approximately four hours. As Nan called us in for lunch, I ignored my mother's instruction to bring the car onto the veranda and paid the ultimate price when it got pinched from the front yard within minutes. Inconceivable behaviour from the thief on Christmas of all days, but this was part and parcel of living in South Melbourne at the time. The follow-up gift was not nearly as pleasant as my mother delivered a perfectly timed slap across my arse.

Notwithstanding the horrific living conditions and the appalling role modelling of my parents, aunts and uncles, I absolutely loved Nan and Pop Aghan. Despite the hand they'd been dealt with, they tried so hard to make it work for all of us.

While I also can't remember ever receiving kisses, hugs, or any form of affection from either of them, I was the one kid who had a relationship with them. My grandmother was an angel. Edith was the matriarch holding the family together and it's of no surprise I had more of a relationship with her than with any other woman in the family. She was born in Norong (near Rutherglen) but her inclination for helping others was no doubt related to her Scottish blood – the friendly fucking Scots.

Pop was very much the same when it came to opening the house up and looking out for others. Like my father, Old Sam was a hard worker, driving half-jinkers for the South Melbourne Council and picking up rubbish. It wasn't the most glamorous job, but it served a purpose. If I wasn't helping Dad at the stables, I would usually ride along with Old Sam.

Every night, without fail, Old Sam would sit by the fire with a bottle of stout. While my uncles would take a collection of gallon jars down to the local and get them refilled, occasionally knocking off 12 gallons of beer at a time, my grandfather would never indulge the golden ale. He was stout through and through. Like most kids growing up in Australia, he would give me a sip of his drink before I realised how shit it tasted. It's not the only reason I haven't been an alcohol enthusiast throughout my life, but it certainly didn't whet my appetite.

I'll never forget the night Old Sam died and the sound of Nan screaming.

Something's happened to Sam.

He had gone to the toilet earlier in the night but had never made it back, with my father finding his body lying outside the front door after suffering a heart attack. We were so young and struggled to comprehend what had happened. In the weeks thereafter, I repeatedly asked Nan where Sam was but received no response. As it turned out, she passed away the following year and I lost both grandparents in less than 12 months.

EDITH & OLD SAM

Just days after Old Sam's death, one of the biggest incidents of my childhood occurred. Uncle Arthur had been stealing petrol and storing it in a 44-gallon drum next to the back laundry. Fucking shock. More foolishly, however, he'd been storing it near the chip heater. While he'd normally tighten the bung on the drum, he failed to do so that day and allowed fumes to escape and fill the immediate vicinity. Without any knowledge of petrol fumes or the damage that can be caused when exposed to flames, I unsuspectingly lit a rolled-up piece of paper to ignite the heater. As I waved the paper in an attempt to put it out, embers hit the fumes and caused an explosion that would ultimately destroy the home. My father, who was standing just a few feet away, was blown face-first through a plate glass window. He suffered severe burns and deep cuts from the blast, while Uncle Athol – who was also nearby – received burns to his legs. Both were rushed to Prince Henry Hospital in a serious condition. By some small miracle, I only endured superficial burns of my own, but I was admitted to hospital with my father, nonetheless. The incident was widely reported in newspapers throughout Australia, with the house completely gutted, destroying almost all our possessions, and leaving us homeless.

> **Two Burnt When Petrol Drum Explodes**
>
> MELBOURNE, Sunday.—An explosion at South Melbourne yesterday damaged a home and severely burned two brothers.
>
> A spark from a wood-burning copper ignited fumes from a 44-gallon petrol drum a few feet away.
>
> The explosion wrecked the building, an old two-storey timber house, and flames destroyed bedding and furniture in six rooms.
>
> Lawrence Agban (36) had his arm burnt, and an artery was gashed as he smashed a window to escape. Athol Agban (26) had his legs burnt.
>
> Both are in Prince Henry's Hospital in a serious condition.

(CREDIT: NATIONAL LIBRARY OF AUSTRALIA)

The South Melbourne community rallied around us eight kids on the Saturday of the fire, ensuring we each had somewhere to stay by nightfall. The others were billeted out to relatives and family friends, while I went to live with the Lumby's. Both were heavily involved with the Salvation Army and knew my father from Mr Lumby's work driving a horse and cart. Having two children of their own, Wally and Alfie, the Lumby's were what I considered a proper family and provided me with my first-ever sense of parental care.

After 12 months in hospital and another year getting back on his feet, my father brought us together again when he rented a home in Bay Street, Port Melbourne. It was the happiest time of my childhood. For the first two months, we were all back together as kids and in our own house. Unfortunately, like most of the positive memories from those days, it was only fleeting.

My father was always the same. His biggest fault was that he just kept drinking and it meant we had no money for food, clothes, or basic healthcare. My mother wouldn't come home for days at a time while Dad was away working, and it only served to fuel our assumptions that she was having an affair. Before we knew it, the arguments, the swearing, and the beatings had all started up again.

Not before long, the local Methodist Mission were made aware of our situation. They, with the Health Department, stepped in and deemed our parents unfit to look after us. The Mission organised alternative living arrangements for us, with Lennie, Joy and I shipped off to the Melbourne Orphanage. It was there, at Windermere, my next childhood nightmare began.

2
THE ORPHANAGE

'It's not whether you get knocked down;
it's whether you get up.'
VINCE LOMBARDI, GREEN BAY PACKERS.

AT THAT POINT IN my life, the pearly whites had not seen a lot of sun. Luckily, the South Melbourne Methodist Mission had established themselves as a 'haven of refuge upon those whom fortune has not smiled' during the post-depression era. Their role as a pillar of physical and emotional support was well-known throughout the community, so when they came knocking and relocated us to the Melbourne Orphanage, we experienced a rare sense of anticipation and excitement. Maybe fortune was about to greet us with a handshake and a big cheeky grin?

Formerly known as the Melbourne Orphan Asylum, the Orphanage was officially established in 1926 at 'Windemere' in Brighton. It originally accommodated orphans from 3-16 years of age, but after World War II, expanded its intake of children to include those from 'broken homes'. I never knew what 'broken homes' meant, but I assumed an alcoholic father, disconnected mother and uncles and aunts who committed sin for breakfast fell under the 'broken' umbrella.

By the time Lennie, Joy and I were considered damaged enough and admitted in the late 1940s, it became clear the provision of care for its members was secondary to the Orphanage's focus on discipline. Serious discipline. Discipline that I would consider as a coach of young men later in life, but never enact. You'd think about it, but you'd never do it. That kind of discipline.

Situated on the same site as the Brighton Beach State School, the Orphanage sat on prime bayside real estate. It consisted of an administration block, a series of large two-story cottages, and a shoe shop. Each cottage had dormitories capable of housing 40 children in single beds and a bath in the centre of the room. I'd never seen anything like it. You need only look at photos to admire the administration building's aesthetic magnificence. After the living conditions at Coventry Street, arriving at the Orphanage was like walking through the front gates of Camelot. And the sun was beaming down on my teeth.

THE ORPHANAGE WITH ITS CAMELOT VIBE

The first person I met at Windemere was Mr J.C. Butler – the Secretary Superintendent. An officious looking man, he never entered the public arena without his collar, tie, and waistcoat. As the author of *'The first hundred years, being a brief history of the Melbourne Orphanage from 1851-1951'*, Mr Butler was considered the Godfather of the Orphanage and watched countless children walk through its doors during his 33 years in charge. His longevity was undoubtedly a result of his dedication to the profession and his ability to maintain a firm sense of control in almost any situation. It was a dictatorship, but for the right reasons.

Like most benevolent dictators, however, there was always another side to him – a Mr Hyde to his Dr Jekyll. An arsehole to his gentlemen. He was careful that we didn't see his 'other' side often, but when he did lose his temper, it was to great effect. It was his own version of white line fever, except his line referred to certain behavioural standards rather than stepping onto a football field. Nevertheless, the result was the same; if a line was crossed, you knew about it. Butler's weapon of choice was a small thin cane and when he decided to use it, he'd slice it across your hamstrings with expert speed and precision.

Far out Mr Butler, that really hurts.

I can keep this up all day, Lawrence.

The smiles that fortune brought us were short-lived as the Orphanage arranged to separate Lennie, Joy, and I into different cottages. I was housed at Cottage No. 2 and would only see my brother and sister during visiting hours each Saturday. It was certainly a tough pill to swallow at the time, but after meeting one of our House Mothers, I soon felt a great sense of eldest sibling relief for the other two.

While Mr Butler was Jekyll, Hyde and Overlord of Windemere, each individual cottage was under the primary care of two House Mothers employed to oversee its day-to-day operations.

One of our 'carers' was Miss Hawkins. Now, it's hard to describe someone so callous without sounding like I have a serious chip on my shoulder, but I'll give it a crack. And I won't even use the 'b' word.

Hawkins was a cruel and vindictive woman who I could only assume projected her own anger and sadness onto others. Namely me. She was roughly 50 years old, incredibly unattractive and could be easily identified via a large mole on her left cheek. That hairy mole. It makes me shudder just thinking about how often I saw it when we had our one-on-one 'meetings'. Hawkins was defined by her beliefs on law and order and patrolled the corridors like a Gestapo, imposing rules and punishments to suit her own agenda.

She had her favourites in Cottage No. 2 and it's safe to say I was not one of them. It was likely because of my grandfather's Chinese blood that was running through my veins, but she took an instant displeasure and maintained it for the three years I was at Windemere.

For those children who were blacklisted by Hawkins – lucky me, I wasn't the only one – she would hand out punishments with The Strap. Of all the beatings I copped from my father, Mr Butler, Camp Pell, and the local gangs of South Melbourne, nothing came close to the pain I felt when Hawkins wielded The Strap. Tucked into her pinafore like a samurai sword, it was a two-inch-wide leather strap with a wooden handle. Like its owner, it was unimpressive to the eye, but its mere existence gave her overinflated sense of importance another few inches.

The Strap-happy Hawkins didn't need a lot of evidence to

warrant its use. She only required proof of minor infractions: talking in bed of a night-time, unpolished shoes, an untidy collar or mismatching the buttons on your shirt.

What have I told you about that darned collar, Lawrence?

I'll fix it now Miss.

Too late, you can fix it in my office you little cretin.

While she may have been ugly, she wasn't stupid. To hide the welts on our skin, she would make us lean against a wardrobe with our arms stretched out and unleash two swats across our triceps.

What about my legs Miss? Can you hit my legs?

Don't be silly Lawrence and put your jumper on before you leave.

I hadn't quite starting using the f-word to this point of my life but fuck it would've got a workout these days.

The Strap would occasionally bring tears to my eyes, but I tried to respond by gritting my teeth and staring her down. Even back then, I wasn't in the habit of showing enemies any weakness. Fuck that. Of course, there were times when my self-restraint was not quite as rock-solid, and I screamed in agony. It did little to stop the punishment or elicit any kind of compassion and often resulted in one or two extras. Forever the smartarse, there were some days when I actually questioned her ability to physically abuse children.

FOOTY THE GREAT LEVELLER

Is that the best you've got Miss?

Coincidentally, they were also the days when two hits quickly turned into five or six.

While I received the most attention from Hawkins, she reserved a certain level of disdain for two other children, Billy Skilbeck and Billy McIntosh. I slept alongside Billy S in the dormitory and soon realised he'd developed a habit of pissing the bed. Not good. According to Hawkins, Billy's bladder issues were my fault. She accused me of keeping him awake all night talking and because he was scared to go to the toilet in the dark, I was at fault when he woke up swimming in his own piss. I always dreaded morning bed inspections when Hawkins was on duty.

Billy's sheets are wet, Lawrence. You're coming with me.

Unfortunately, this wasn't the only situation where urine caused me distress in Cottage No. 2. It's hard to believe there'd be a hierarchical system imposed among children in an orphanage, but there was. And it was never more obvious than on bath night. Once a week, kids took it in turns bathing in groups of 10 at a time. Unsurprisingly, Hawkins would allow her favourites to bathe first. Warm water, soap, maybe even a bit of shampoo and conditioner for those who were that way inclined. Not for us. By the time me and the two Billys were ordered to wash, the unchanged water was freezing cold, there was no soap left and the bath was filled with the piss of the 30 other kids. Billy S was basically cleaning his own urine off him with the urine of others.

Group dinners were much the same. Hawkins acted as the security guard for the dining room and made certain those of us she disliked were the last to enter. How good do you think the food was when we got to the front of the queue?

The only respite we had from Hawkins' mistreatment was school. The advantage of living so close to Brighton Beach State School was the education we received as children of the Orphanage. Every morning, we'd eat breakfast, dress in our uniform, and take the short walk from our cottage to school. While I never excelled inside the classroom, attending the State School gave me the chance to form a relationship with footy, with games of kick-to-kick and markers-up a regular occurrence.

Special character imparted by the presence of orphans. Friendships were formed, but the camaraderie of the children at Windemere distinguished them. - Brighton Beach State School Centenary History (1978).

Despite the happier memories we created at school, it all got a bit much for us one day – The Strap, the abuse, the piss-soaked baths – so two of us decided to run away from the Orphanage. We had no money, no knowledge of the area and no plan so it was no surprise when our gallant efforts to escape were thwarted by the time we reached Brighton Beach. The senior boys from the school were sent after us and when they delivered their catch to Butler and Hawkins, we received a special edition of The Strap and The Cane. A very special, week-long edition.

For three hours on a Saturday afternoon from 2-5pm, visitors were allowed at the Orphanage. Rain, hail, or snow, we were made to sit on the bench outside the main office with a bag of 12 all-coloured toffees to share with our visitors. If nobody came to see you, the lollies weren't to be touched. In the three years we spent at Windemere, Lennie, Joy and I never had one visitor.

No parent, no family friends, nobody. My mother and father had separated by that point. While she was gallivanting around as though her eight children didn't exist, he was toiling away at work. Unfortunately, this meant there was no time in their schedules to visit the three of us. So, by 5.01pm every Saturday, if there weren't 12 toffees in our lolly bags, our legs were going to face off with The Cane. Can you imagine how difficult it was to stay out of the lolly bag? The Cane was often worth it.

I believe I survived the Orphanage ordeal because of a refusal to accept physical abuse. Because I was willing to look Hawkins in the eye with every strike of The Strap. With every hit I received, it was just another chance to get back up and go again.

In a sense, I was lucky that I had the security of a bed, a meal, and some sort of education. Irrespective of what I'd been through, as I laid my head on the pillow at the end of each day, I knew it was certainly a lot better than living at home.

So, when the Orphanage contacted my father and informed him of its closure and the need to find us alternative living arrangements, the question had to be asked; was it going to be the same as last time? Surely it would mean less piss. At the very least.

3

CAMP PELL & SOUTH MELBOURNE TECH

Rocky: 'You know, I been lucky.
Somebody up there likes me.'

Norma: 'Somebody down here, too.'

SINCE THE RELEASE OF Rocky Graziano's biopic *Somebody Up There Like Me (1956)*, the film has always served as inspiration to me while facing life's endless list of challenges. Rocky's plight, his experiences, his attitude towards life and his relationships; I connected with it all. Whether it be family, playing football, coaching, or my professional career, I've praised my luck on more than one occasion.

Paul Newman's character was consistently abused by his drunk-as-a-skunk father throughout childhood, leading to a total disregard for authority and careless behaviour in the face of the law. He did what he wanted, and he did not give a flying fuck about the consequences. It wasn't until he met his wife, Norma, that he figured out what he did and didn't want to be. While world champion boxer isn't on the cards for most men trying to find their way in the world, finding a woman who motivates you is one of life's great gifts. Whatever path you take.

As a prelude to the following few chapters, there are many similarities between Rocky's story and mine. It's not just the fact that a young Laurie Aghan thought all cops were scumbags, but it includes boxing as a path to inclusion and the gang mentality in the slums. Above all else, they sure as shit chose the lead actor appropriately - I'm sure my wife Lorna wakes up and momentarily forgets that it's me, and not Paul Newman, breathing heavily down her neck.

On the topic of facing challenges and building character, the next was an absolute fucking doozie. If the challenge of Miss Hawkins and the Orphanage, in addition to the baptism of fire (literally) I faced at Coventry Street, wasn't enough for one childhood, living at Camp Pell undoubtedly gave me the confidence to face whatever life threw at me.

Our time at the Orphanage had come to an end and they contacted my father and told him to organise alternative accommodation for Lennie, Joy, and myself. He was still in no position to care for three children, so he instead sent us to live with Uncle Billy and Aunt Phyllis at Camp Pell.

Like most traumatic events, Melbourne has done its utmost to forget the memory of 'Camp Hell'. There has been an odd feature article in the rags over the years, but many of those who never experienced the poverty and criminal activity that took place are dead set ignorant of its history. Now I'm about to take you on a brief history lesson of mid-twentieth century

Melbourne because I feel it's important to give context to Camp Pell and how it came to be before spiraling into notoriety. Well, for those who know about it. The rest of you, strap in.

Situated at Royal Park in Parkville, the area was used as a temporary army camp during both world wars. Following the events of Pearl Harbor and the United States' one-way ticket into WWII, 250,000 Americans were stationed there in pyramid tents and Nissen huts. In February 1942, Major Floyd J. Pell became the first American airman killed on active service in Australia. He was defending Darwin against a Japanese air attack and for that, the area was named in his honour. Camp Pell was officially born.

It wasn't long before the Camp began to develop a reputation. An unsavoury one. Just three months after Major Pell's death, the Brownout murders took place nearby. Over the course of 15 days, Private Edward Leonski became one of the most feared serial killers in Melbourne after he murdered three women. One of his victims, Gladys Hosking, was found just 350 metres from Royal Park. Dubbed the 'Brownout Strangler', Leonski was captured in Camp Pell, court-martialled, and hanged liked a freshly washed towel. From that moment, his actions left a mark on the area that laid the foundation for criminal behaviour for more than a decade.

When the war ended in 1945 and the American forces at Camp Pell returned home, the area was repurposed to house around 3,000 people affected by the post-war housing shortage. Many Melburnians needed emergency accommodation following evictions enforced by slum reclamation policies. The stopgap solution was the soldier-appropriate but family-unfriendly conditions at Royal Park. The government's answer was to place vulnerable people in the area haunted by the Brownout Strangler. It was bound to fail. And I was right in the middle of it.

At the same time the Victorian politicians were kicking families out of their homes, my father's brother, Billy, and his partner, Phyllis, moved down from Ballarat. Billy was working as the Foreman at Chalmers Transport Company and because of its proximity to Camp Pell, they settled on Area 8.

Billy and Phyllis were trying to build their own life in the city, so they were understandably reluctant to take on three pseudo-orphans. In true Aghan fashion, however, they eventually agreed. For two pounds a week. At least I knew what I was worth.

There were really no living conditions that could surprise me at that point in my life, but the Nissen huts and Area 8 provided another set of challenges. Shaped like an igloo and made from half-cylinders of corrugated steel – the huts were freezing in winter and boiling in summer. Our igloo had three bedrooms, a small lounge and kitchen, an outside toilet, and showers that I used once every two to three weeks. Each numbered area had 40 to 50 igloos lined up within an arm's length of each other. It was cramped but otherwise provided a communal feel to the whole living-in-severe-poverty and fuck-my-life experience.

Without question, the worst aspect of Camp Pell was the crime. There was always something happening. The dictionary would describe it as rape, assault, infanticide, stabbings, and robbery. All the time. Drunken criminals would frequent the area and cause mayhem, often attacking women as they arrived home from work.

As I got to know the other kids in Area 8, we decided to take the law into our own hands. We formed a vigilante group to protect the young girls and elderly women who got off the last tram of the night. That was the predator tram. There were seven of us kids and I was the ringleader. Each night, when the tram stopped on its route from Sydney Road through to Mt Alexander Road, we'd wait with wooden fence pickets in our hands, meet the women and guide them safely back to their huts. It was often enough to deter the would-be criminals; a bunch of kids who had no concern for their own safety.

Of course, it didn't always go to plan and there were times when we'd be required to use our weapon of choice. One night, I noticed movement in the distance and the high-pitched screams of a woman 150m away. As I picked up my fence picket and ran toward her, I realised a man was kicking her repeatedly as she lay helpless on the ground. The others in the group followed my lead and, without giving a blow-by-blow recap of the brawl, we certainly didn't hold back. I'd be surprised if that prick ever walked again.

The Argus newspaper promulgated Camp Pell's closure in 1953, describing its survival as 'a disgrace to Melbourne and a measure of the failure of government in Victoria' and referring to it as a 'squalid sinkhole'. A squalid sinkhole? There are only one or two superlatives missing from that description.

When the city's dirty little secret was finally abolished in 1955 ahead of the Olympics, we were long gone. Billy and Phyllis had given up on their attempt to create a life in the city and returned to Ballarat, while we fell back into the Aghan clan.

I never gave a lot of thought to Camp Pell. I was more than happy to try and let my memories of it fade into occasional bad dreams. This was until I was playing footy at Sandringham years later and a man introduced himself to me as Billy Archer.

You don't know who I am,
but I lived with you as a kid in Area 8.

FOOTY THE GREAT LEVELLER

You poor bastard. You poor, poor bastard.

Do you ever think about it?

Not one fucking bit, mate.

When Uncle Billy and Phyllis left Camp Pell, my father rented a room on Raglan Street in Albert Park and asked me to move in with him. Irrespective of our past, this was a positive and I was looking forward to it. But while it reignited my bond with Laurie Sr, it momentarily ended my relationship with Lennie and Joy as they went and lived with other families. We'd endured The Orphanage and Camp Pell together; I was sure we'd meet again.

Moving back in with my father meant enrolling at South Melbourne Technical School. I remember my first day clearly. Wearing old grey shorts, a pair of sandals and an unironed shirt with two buttons missing, it was a far cry from the red, white, and navy blue worn by every other student. As we were gathered in the quadrangle, with me standing out like the proverbial canine genitalia, the headmaster made a beeline for me. Shit, here we go.

Who are you?

I'm Laurie Aghan, sir.

You look like a dog's breakfast, come with me.

Dog's breakfast, dog's balls, it's safe to say I wasn't hitting the right fashion notes. He pulled me out from the group and led me upstairs to their version of an op-shop and fitted me out with second-hand clothes and a peaked cap. Not the ideal start.

I struggled to make friends in the early days at the Tech School and I cannot remember joining in for one game of allies. The first time I properly engaged with other students was at the Technical Schools Boxing and Wrestling Night at the South Melbourne Town Hall.

Despite the altercations I'd been in at Camp Pell, I was never interested – or had trained for that matter – in either boxing or wrestling. These somewhat important facts didn't seem to bother my form master, Mr Dave Morrison, who told me to bring my runners, shorts, and a sweatshirt to the event. He'd already decided I would be the emergency for both disciplines.

You probably won't be called because the bouts are settled, Aghan.

I hope not, Mr Morrison. I don't know how to do it either. Well, not properly.

I got the call-up within 10 minutes of setting foot in the hall. A boy had been hurt while wrestling earlier in the night and I was to fill his spot. Of course, I had never properly wrestled a day in my life. I got absolutely fucking belted.

Battered and bruised from my less-than-impressive debut, I hadn't even made it to the stools at the back of the Hall before I heard Morrison call for me again. The kid who was fixtured to fight Kenny Boyd for the Technical Schools Heavyweight Boxing Championship hadn't turned up. I wonder why. As the first emergency, I was required to try and go three rounds with South Melbourne FC's future ruckman.

FOOTY THE GREAT LEVELLER

You're fighting Kenny Boyd.

Sir, have you seen the size of him? He'll kill me.

Kenneth John Boyd went on to become one of the more infamous operators to pull on a Swans jumper. He was the type of player feared by the opposition and idolised by the fans. After winning two flags with the South's Thirds in 1955 and 1956, Boyd was selected as the first-choice ruck for the seniors and played 60 games over the next five seasons. He didn't miss almost two years' worth of games over that period because he was injury-prone or out of form. No, in his five seasons, Boyd missed 30 matches due to suspension. His reputation and playing style epitomised South's – rough. Fucking rough. In fact, after receiving a six-match suspension following two separate incidents against Carlton's John Heathcote and John Nicholls in 1961, he followed it up with a 12-week ban in the return-match at Princes Park later that season after flooring Nicholls. This is the bloke they called 'Big Nick' and Kenny had, without hesitation, put the future Hall of Famer on his arse. And this was who I was poised to fight in my first bout?

While he still had some growing to do before starring for the Swans, Kenny was already 13.8 stone on the night of the fight, almost three stone heavier than me. When we entered the ring and sized each other up, he looked about 6'10 and I was doing everything I could to not shit my pants. Not sure the op-shop had a replacement for that.

When the bell rang for the opening round and the 500-strong crowd started roaring, I knew I just had to try and last. Kenny knocked me down twice in the first round and Morrison, only now realising the danger I was in, asked me if I wanted him to stop the fight.

No, he hasn't hurt me.

Kenny knocked me down another two times over the second and third rounds, but I just kept getting up. It hurt, but not enough to keep me down. At one stage toward the end of the fight, I thought I really got on top of him and that I might be able to finish him. I didn't and I couldn't. He was far too big and strong. But I lasted three rounds and returned to my corner physically and mentally exhausted.

Why did you do that, Mr Morrison? Why do you hate me?

Mate, I don't hate you at all.
You were phenomenal out there.

Morrison had tears in his eyes. What was going on? It was uncharacteristic of him to be emotional, but it told me he was proud of my performance and that was exciting. In later years, I ran into former South Melbourne Mayor and fellow Tech student, Reg Macey, who explained that Dave Morrison was a war hero. That news gave the post-fight moment yet another layer of significance.

Unsurprisingly, Kenny won the fight. But that boxing match changed everything for me. Living so close to school, I was often the first student to arrive, and I'd pass the time by playing my own game of allies. After that fight though, like a happy ending to a soppy film, a group of kids approached me and asked if I wanted to join them. It wasn't a boxing movie about the world middleweight champion, but I thought for the very first time, maybe somebody up there does like me.

4
LIFE IN SOUTH MELBOURNE

'You may have to fight a battle more than once to win it.'

MARGARET THATCHER,

FORMER PRIME MINISTER OF THE UNITED KINGDOM.

MY SCHOOL LIFE WAS short-lived. Despite making friends on the back of my fight with Kenny Boyd, I'd started wandering around the streets of South Melbourne instead of attending class. School just wasn't for me. But as you're about to find out, my life education was about to continue.

Like many students in those days, I started looking for work from a young age. After getting an exemption from my father to leave South Melbourne Tech, I began my professional working career with stints at Monumental Masons, Walpamur Paints, Fleetways Transport, and even as a paperboy.

While working in Walpamur's Port Melbourne warehouse, there was a situation where I inadvertently continued my boxing training. By inadvertent, I mean that I landed one of the all-time right hooks to the Head Foreman's chin. An abusive and argumentative Englishman, he had a habit of standing over his workers and trying to intimidate them to get his way. I'd dealt with dictators in the past and I wasn't going to cop it from him. On what ended up being my last day with the company, he started on me with his offensive and equally unwitty 'useless dog' diatribe.

Within moments, I felt my fist clench and my arm extend as I sent the shit-talking Pommy bastard straight over a pile of paint tins. Absolutely fucking nailed him. He was no Kenny Boyd, but Dave Morrison would have still been proud. Unsurprisingly, once he picked himself up off the floor and gathered his thoughts, he fired me on the spot.

Get out of here, you're done.

My pleasure, dickhead.

Understanding the value of money better than most, it wasn't ideal to lose work. But to see him sprawled out on the ground in a brand-new art smock, fuck it was worth it.

Not long after the Walpamur Ashes experience, my father, who was shunting railway trucks at both the wharf and Spencer Street Railway Yard, took me in to work with him. The most enjoyable part of working with Laurie Senior was our lunch breaks with Tom Sheedy at the Markillies Hotel. They were easily the best meals I'd had, and Tom often shouted me a raspberry and lemonade cordial. I got to know the father of Richmond and Essendon legend, Kevin Sheedy, well during those lunches.

Years later, I recounted the shunting days when I spoke to Kevin at Hassa Mann's AFL Hall of Fame induction in Canberra.

FOOTY THE GREAT LEVELLER

I had only met him briefly before that night while he was playing at Richmond. At the time, I was leading an Old Scotch training session at Yarra Park and when the Tigers attempted to kick us off the ground for their own training purposes, I politely told him to find someone else to fellate.

Get fucked.

I doubled down when he offered us a pair of new Sherrins if we left, carefully explaining that they'd be of better use inside his stool passage.

Shove it up your arse, Sheeds.

Thankfully, Hassa's induction and the topic of our fathers at the railways resulted in a far more amicable meeting the second time around. It couldn't have really been any worse.

It was during this time when I was helping my father that I began working casually for Fleetways, shovelling coal at General Motors Holden in Fisherman's Bend. It was a tough, character-building job where we were required to work through extremely harsh conditions. Whether it be pelting down with rain or unrelenting heat, you worked your arse off to get the quotas done for the day. Eventually, this took its toll on me, and I suffered a life-threatening bout of rheumatic fever. More details can be found on this period of my life later in the book, but suffice to say, I was in bad shape.

My life didn't improve for a while thereafter as I was forced to embrace the South Melbourne slums. I was constantly on the lookout for trouble and, just as importantly, food. I was a rapidly growing ruckman-in-waiting and had the appetite to boot.

Luckily, Wednesdays and Fridays were covered with fruit. Or the bruised leftovers of what were once distinguishable pieces of fruit, to be more specific. Johnny and May Marmo operated a fruit stall at the South Melbourne Market, and they would package the unused pieces for me.

In the early days of running around South Melbourne, I remember a short Chinese man, Ken Cheng, who carried a cradle of wood across his shoulders with two stainless steel bins full of dim sims and chicken rolls. He walked around to all the factories in South Melbourne, and we'd wait at the Southern Cross Hotel in Cecil Street to make sure we didn't miss out on a couple of dimmies.

His stall, which was based at the Market, opened in 1949 and quickly became the most sought-after venue for dim sims in Melbourne. People would come from all parts of Victoria after hearing of these steaming pockets of gold. When Ken died in 2006, his daughter Lily was quoted as saying her father believed his dim sims were the best in the world. Have you had a South Melbourne dim sim? Ken wasn't wrong, let me assure you.

Cheng's dim sims weren't the only popular item in South Melbourne at the time, with Spiro and Mickey Christopher's fish cakes also a market leader. On Friday nights I would venture down to their fish and chip shop and part with two bob for one. I knew Spiro from my occasional attendance at school where I'd often sit next to him and cheat off his work. I only stopped looking over his shoulder when I realised he was thicker than me. I loved him, but he was as dumb as a fucking doorknob.

Both Spiro and Mickey knew about my family life and how rough I was living, so each time I'd order a fish cake they'd throw in four bobs' worth of chips. It was their way of looking after me. Like Johnny and May Marmo, I had allies in South Melbourne.

FOOTY THE GREAT LEVELLER

Like most local areas, we had our fair share of characters. They were considered a part of the furniture and with God as my witness, they were entertaining. Steamroller Ron would chase the rollers out of the South Melbourne Council while blowing his whistle and waving his white hanky, while Jacky Wales and Gino Romeo would sit on the park bench and drink flagons of wine, abusing anyone who refused to give them money.

Oi kid, got any spare change?

Nah, sorry Jacky.

Well piss off then you little shit.

Ultimately, they were all harmless. Mental. But harmless.

It was during this time that the youth subculture of bodgies and widgies had made its way from NSW. Little gangs formed around South and Port Melbourne, causing havoc by breaking windows and stealing anything that wasn't nailed down. If you haven't heard about the bodgies and widgies, just imagine the Greaser culture in the United States – it was a direct rip-off.

> What with "bodgies" growing their hair long and getting around in satin shirts, and "wedgies" cutting their hair short and wearing jeans, confusion seems to be arising about the sex of some Australian adolescents.
> The Sydney Morning Herald (1951).

Victoria Police, headed by Sergeant Jim Macklewain, formed a Bodgies and Widgies Squad to control (eliminate) the gangs. Ruthless Jim was the big kahuna at South Melbourne Police and operated by the adage that two's company and three's a crowd.

I'm not entirely sure how successful Jim was taking on the 'folk devils of the fifties'. But if you were ever caught in a group of two or more with your hair slicked back and a kiss curl hanging down your forehead, you'd end up with a foot so far up your arse you could taste his shoe polish. I can confirm it tasted like shit.

While he wasn't my favourite part of the furniture around South Melbourne, I heeded Jim's warnings and accepted a job selling newspapers on Eastern Road. The only issue was the number of crooks in the area, many of whom would steal the little money we made trading Heralds and Sporting Globes and threaten violence if we said anything. It was fucking tough.

This is how my life was. It was one battle after another. But as the former British Prime Minister said, you may have to fight a battle more than once to win it. I was fighting, but I'm not sure how often I was winning.

5

WORKING LIFE

> 'You can fix the pokies, nobble a horse and even drug a runner,
> but you can't argue the toss.'
> **LIONEL 'NAPPY' OLLINGTON.**

AS WE TAKE A closer look at my professional life over the years, I need to start by acknowledging the impact of Lionel Ollington.

Some will remember 'Nappy' from his short VFL stint with Footscray, where he managed five games in 1953 in between a storied career with Montague Rovers. However, many more will remember the two-up king, known for his less-than-legal operation and rubbing shoulders with prominent Melbourne identities such as Tony Mokbel and Mick Gatto. While he failed to get it permanently legalised in Australia, Nappy was the reason there are two-up games once a year on Anzac Day. His famous Flemington Racecourse games are still operating to this day.

My association with the king started at Lagoon Oval where I used to run messages for Nappy at his two-up games, earning three quid for my efforts. Looking back, I can see how I fitted into the scene so seamlessly with plenty of money to be made and authorities to be disregarded.

After running messages for a while, Nappy invited me to work with him on the Wharf as his gang's amenities man. More money and more time around Nappy? Yes please.

Unfortunately, looking after the gang's personal belongings wasn't exactly a full-time job and the inconsistency of the work left me in the same financial position that I had grown up in. I needed more.

How can I get more permanent work, Nappy?

I'll make a few calls, but you'll need to submit yourself to the boys. And that can go either way.

Fuck it, I'm in. Whatever it takes.

As always, Nappy delivered. The following day I was standing in the middle of a circle of hardened old wharfies and praying for a 100% vote to get the job. It was Leading Teams before its time, but with gangsters, boxers, and bikies.

To this day I have no idea what was asked or how I responded, but I successfully navigated the scariest inquisition known to man and was appointed as a floater – one who makes up the gang shortage if a wharfie falls sick or takes leave.

I loved my time on the wharf and, more importantly, I loved the blokes I worked with. The wharfies cared for each other unlike anything I had seen to that point in my life. In many ways, they were like a football team; you don't always see eye-to-eye, but you always look after one another, you work hard, and you celebrate together. No wharfie ever missed out. If someone was hurt or in need of money for any reason, donations were made every Thursday when the cash cart came around. It was always quick to fill up.

With great leaders such as Teddy Bull and Claude Cumberlege, no job was ever too big or too small for those gangs. Some tasks were dog shit, don't get me wrong. From loading maggot-infested sheep skin bags to working through arctic conditions until the job was done, the working conditions could be a unions' worst nightmare. But you did what it took and never complained.

One night after a few too many beverages, we were loading a batch of Holden cars in the shipping yard. I was driving the yard truck but soon realised I needed to use the toilet.

They've gone straight through me; I need to drain the trouser snake boys.

No worries, Abs. We'll wait.

You'd better. No stuffing around.

After leaving the truck in neutral while I was relieving myself, I felt a sudden jolt and heard three loud banging noises followed by muffled laughter and someone screaming.

For God's sake.

When I returned, I was greeted by four completely and utterly totalled Holdens and one foreman losing his mind. Thankfully, those on duty agreed to blame the incident on the movement of the ship, leaving out the whole 'the lads were pissed as newts' story.

From devaluing Holden cars to procuring new ski jumpers, transistor radios, cartons of beer and pallets of whisky, we had a lot of fun on the wharf. And we got away with just about everything.

Percy Mayes – whose son, Johnny, you will read more about throughout this book – was one of the gang leaders. The man was unmissable in his white peaked hat and athletic build, but he was as tight as a fish's arsehole. Every time one worked in his gang, you had to pay two bob for a cup of tea. Two fucking bob. I basically funded Mayzey's education via my love for a strong chamomile. Despite being a scrooge, Percy typified what it was to be a wharfie: loyal, hardworking, and fiercely dedicated to his family and his mates.

It was during this time that I met my best mate, Reggie Smythe. He too was a leader who one day successfully shanghaied me into joining his gang. What a ride that was. We became inseparable, the two of us.

One of the regular episodes of the Laurie and Reggie Show would air in the late hours of the night following a double header at work. After being rained off the wharf and sent home for the day, Reggie and I would make our way to a particular nightclub in the city.

In those days, there were three or four crowd controllers manning the door. As you can imagine, these weren't small men. Former wrestlers and boxers. The old 'brick shithouse' comes to mind. Irrespective of their above average and intimidating frames, my learned mate Reggie decided to test their mettle one night and after one too many ales. To this day, his words still ring in my half-beaten ears.

Let's see how good these blokes are.

Well fuck me. A full-on brawl broke out between the bouncers and the wharfies, and I'm not ashamed to admit the beforementioned wrestlers and boxers had our measure. Comfortably. Unfortunately, this wasn't a once off on the Laurie and Reggie Show as we regularly traded blows with the bouncers, only to walk back the following night, shake hands and do it all again.

I met many accomplished sportsmen during my time on the wharf, including, champion boxer Hilton Brooks, Kevin Hargreaves, Teddy Nolton, Ron Toohey, and Reggie 'Ox' Earl.

Despite being mates with some of the hardest men in Melbourne, it didn't always keep me out of trouble. In fact, I was so confident with those surrounding me, I often brought it upon myself.

One Saturday morning, a group of us were standing outside the Montague Hotel in Port Melbourne when an old grey jaguar pulled up. A red-faced titan of a man hopped out, looked at me and started to make a few demands. I had no idea who he was, but I wasn't in the mood to take shit from anyone.

> *You, go get a bucket off the publican and wash my fucking car.*

> *Piss off, dickhead.*

It was at this point that he grabbed me by the scruff of the neck with the look of somone who had put one or two blokes like me in hospital before. Realising just how big he was and knowing my own limitations, I quickly got a bucket and washed his *fucking car*. After I had finished the job and he had handed me 20 quid, it was only then I was informed that he was former light-heavyweight boxer, gangster and standover man, John Eric Twist. Or as his CV read, a painter and decorator. Twist was thrown in prison for 18 months after assaulting a police constable with chairs in 1954, so I was relieved I chose to wash his *fucking car* that day.

Other than the occasional run-in with Melbourne's underworld, working on the wharf was one of life's great experiences. Working alongside boxers, bikies, footballers from all codes and even future Labor politicians such as Bunna Walsh, there was never a shortage of learning opportunities. And great mates.

Life on the wharf couldn't last forever. Brian 'Moey' Kerr organised a job at Adam Pest Extermination. Little did I know this gig in pest control would alter my financial position in life so dramatically.

In its simplest form, Moey and I were rat catchers. We performed rodent and pest control for restaurants and large buildings, including cinemas. I make this point specifically because, never in my life have I ever seen so many movies. I had one eye on the rats and one eye on John Wayne. So much so, I became a rat-catching celebrity around those parts.

Hey rat catcher, how are you doing?

They say it with love Lorna, they say it with love.

This all changed when Brian went into business for himself. The Adams directors switched my role to fumigation and relocated me to the strawberry farms in Lilydale. I was required to seal plastic sheeting to the soil using chemicals such as methyl bromide, phosphine, and hydrogen cyanide. It was shit work.

Bernie Hyland was the foreman in charge and it's safe to say, he and I never really hit it off. The work was beyond challenging, the conditions on location were third world and the arguments I had with Bernie were constant. Eventually, something had to break.

You're full of shit Bernie you goose!

You're done, Aghan. Pack up and piss off.

He sacked me on the spot and that was it. Where was the Union in those days?

At this point in my life, I was out of work, living in half a house in Malvern and relying on Lorna as the main bread winner.

The struggle to find work lasted about six months. Lorna, forever looking out for me, noticed a newspaper advertisement for a pest control manager at Houghton & Byrne. It would later be known as Rentakil. After scoring an interview with the Victorian Manager, Max Clarke, at the East Brunswick Head Office, a joke, a compliment, and an hour-long discussion about pest control later, the job was mine. The next chapter of my professional career was underway.

Working out of the Frankston office and under the management of Don Ferguson, I did every filthy job one could imagine. From crawling under houses chasing rats and mice to digging trenches and splitting termite-infested stumps. I had done shit work on the wharf, but this took the cake. It didn't make sense as to why I was handed these types of jobs. There was a lot of *'Why me?'* and *'Fuck this, I'm quitting'*, but Lorna always managed to talk me off the ledge. Don later explained it was all a test because he wanted to ensure I would make the grade. Good bloke, Don. But shit test.

After a few years of digging holes and befriending rodents, I received a phone call from then Victorian Manager, Bruce Sterling, requesting a meeting. Max had since been promoted to Australian Managing Director for Rentakil, but as it would turn out, Bruce had his own redeeming qualities.

Upon arrival at East Brunswick, I was greeted by senior members of the management team, including Max, Bruce, Keith Burrows, and Des Phelan.

> *Do you know why you're here?*

> *Not the slightest clue, Mr Clarke. But before we go any further, I must admit I'm sick of crawling through rat shit every day.*

> *Thought that might be the case.*

Max explained that he understood the hardship I was subject to in my role at Frankston, admitting that those instructions had come directly from him. He called it a professional training regime. In footy terms, I guess it was a pre-season camp. I'd probably describe it slightly differently and with a few more superlatives.

As it turned out, the training had paid off because they offered me a new role as Production Manager at the East Brunswick factory. It was certainly a much bigger role, and I would have a team of 10 working under me. Most importantly, no more rat shit. Where do I sign?

I happily worked as the Production Manager for five years. Houghton & Byrne was officially purchased by Rentakil and an internal restructuring elevated me to the position of Australian Fumigation Manager. Recognised as the biggest pest control and fumigation company in the world, Rentakil wanted a greater stranglehold on the international fumigation market, and I was the man to lead it.

It was an exciting time to be involved with the business. We purchased land in Yarraville and a 60-tonne forklift to assist with the container fumigation, unpacking and storage of goods through the Port of Melbourne.

I was entrusted to set up similar operations in each major port across Australia. We fumigated wheat bunkers, grain storages, large buildings (including Brisbane Parliament House), ships and aeroplanes. It was seven days a week, 365 days a year. Christmas, New Year, you fucking bet. I was a man in demand.

More opportunities opened because of my knowledge of the industry, and I'd often give lectures throughout the country. Down the track, I became a Senior Tafe Lecturer on the subject. No more rat catching, that's for sure.

After 20 of the best years with Rentokil, Elders' Director of Business, Norman Jones, called me out of the blue and offered me a job with the Australian juggernaut. After taking a week to consider the proposal and discussing it with Lorna, I had to accept. It was too good to refuse.

Elders was already a market leader in many areas, but they too wanted to become the biggest and most powerful fumigators in the country. That was where I came in. With my knowledge and their deep pockets, we had an incredible opportunity. It might have made me some enemies at Rentakil, but that was the price of doing business.

My first act in the role was to build the team I wanted. And I wanted those I could trust. Simon Dixon, Bob Rennie, Doug Lane, and Greg Donnison were all recruited from Rentakil. Simon was our Entomologist, Bob led the Commercial Pest Control Division, Doug was Fumigator Supervisor and Greg was one of my Senior Fumigators. I wasn't popular with the old firm, but our business grew overnight. Once again in terminology from the football world, we fucking dominated.

Elders commanded most of my time, but within five years, we were the biggest and the best. Unfortunately, it was short-lived. News broke. A bombshell. Well, for me anyway.

Laurie, Elders has proposed a takeover bid for Carlton and Limited Breweries.

That's fantastic news.

Not exactly. It's been recommended that we sell certain parts of the business and that includes Fumigation and Pest Control.

Ok, who have we been sold to?

...Rentakil.

Fuck.

One of Rentakil's main conditions of the sale was that I wouldn't be required. They wanted the boys I took with me, but unsurprisingly didn't want the guy who poached them.

Thankfully, that proposal was quashed during contract negotiations, and I was offered a new role as Project Manager with the group stationed at Garden Street. It was all bullshit. I was given a Secretary and Finance Controller, but I was required to investigate the transport and services contracts that Elders had entered. It was payback.

After a year in the role, Simon, Bob, Greg, and I met for lunch and suggested we go into business for ourselves. Absolutely. I've had enough of this shit. Exopest Australia was born.

It was the third time I had to create a new business but

this one meant a bit more. All the experience we had in the industry paid off handsomely and I was named Managing Director. Things we needed assistance on, we sought help. Dr John Otton was a prime example, giving us plenty of advice as a qualified entomologist. Wayne Stafford was another in terms of transport management.

We purchased a facility and within three years, Exopest Australia had 40 employees. It certainly helped to know the waterfront and industry people followed you. We quickly became the main players in the field.

Sadly, the early 1980s recession hit us hard, and we were forced to borrow from the bank with interest rates at nearly 20%. The financial stress caused many arguments, jealousy, and pettiness. Trust between us leaders disappeared.

After 15 years together, we made the heart wrenching decision to break the business up and sell it for parts. It was a shame. A huge shame. Ultimately, we became our own worst enemies.

That decision brought about my retirement in May 1985. What a working life. I worked hard, I tried to look after my family, and I never once argued the toss. Nappy would have been proud.

6

THE EARLY YEARS OF FOOTBALL

'The interesting thing about coaching is that you have to trouble the comfortable and comfort the troubled.'

RIC CHARLESWORTH,

FORMER AUSTRALIAN NATIONAL WOMEN'S FIELD HOCKEY COACH.

SO FAR, WE'VE COVERED the important and character-building experiences throughout my childhood. In accordance with the game I love, the first quarter is over. And I'm down on the scoreboard. It was a physical opening term; the opposition got the ascendancy but there's no doubting I learnt a lot.

Now, it's time to start throwing my weight around and regain some control in Q2. It's time to start playing footy. While lessons were learnt in my early days as a child, what I got from footy was another level of education.

My junior football journey began when I was 15 years old, and I soon made it a part-time job with three games every weekend. I had always kicked the footy with mates in the streets of South

Melbourne – sometimes made from scrunched-up paper that wouldn't sail any further than 20 yards – but to that point I had never played competitively.

In all, I played over 100 games for five different junior clubs: Beacon Rovers (Under 18s), South United, Waterside Workers, South Melbourne Districts and Montague Rovers.

The Beacon Rovers was the first team I ever played for and as a 15-year-old against men three years older than me, the lessons came thick and fast. As with other aspects of my life, playing with the older kids fast-tracked my maturity and certainly forced me to grow up at an accelerated pace.

But it was during my time with Montague Rovers, at 17, that I experienced one of life's toughest lessons. As Caroline Wilson later described it, I was a semi-invalid. You can read Caroline's article at the end of this chapter, but for now, I'll describe the experience in greater detail.

I was working a casual job at Fleetways Transport at the time and, as I said in the previous chapter, it was shit and demanding work. Remember the whole rain, hail, or shine thing? Whatever it took to hit the quota for the day. After four months, I noticed all my joints started to swell. The pain was unbearable. Most thought it was gout. I wish it was. I continued to work through the pain until it all got too much, and one day I eventually collapsed.

After extensive testing from Scotch-educated doctors, Dr Neil Mackie and Dr Doug Callister, I was diagnosed with rheumatic carditis. These days, Google will tell you that it is a condition in which the heart valves have been permanently damaged by rheumatic fever. The heart valve damage may start shortly after untreated streptococcal infection such as strep throat or scarlet fever.

What I can tell you is that it was fucking excruciating.

I spent one year in Prince Henry's Hospital, often with a canopy over my bed to stop the blankets from resting on my joints. Despite entering hospital at 11.8 stone and as fit as a fiddle, I was prescribed steroids which ultimately caused me to balloon out to 17 stone. My footy and boxing physique disappeared as fast as my ability to walk, and I ended up looking like Buddha. A fat Nepalese prince of prayer.

The most concerning aspect of the entire ordeal was the advice I received from the medical experts, saying I would never play competitive sport again. Predictably, my response centred around '*Bullshit!*' and '*No fucking way!*'

When I finally left hospital after 12 months, I had the assistance of Mrs Lumby, Stella and Dan Manson, and Anna and Tony Bogdanoff. I was so morbidly obese that I could hardly fend for myself. The love and care I received from this group was nothing short of amazing. It really reiterated the meaning of family and parenting.

The return to fighting weight was a slow burn. I started with beach walks into jogging and back into walks again. The comeback changed very quickly when I ran into former street fighter and amateur boxer, Hilton Brooks, and one of his students, Clarrie Williams. Without trying to be a smartarse, Hilton pulled no punches.

Why are you so big?

Excuse me? I've been sick. But I'm trying to lose the weight.

If I trained you (boxing), would you stick at it?

Bloody oath I would.

And just like that, I joined Hilton at the gym every week. The weight fell off me. Within 12 months, I had lost five stone and was not just back to my playing weight, but I was fitter, stronger and could throw a much deadlier left hook.

While I did start playing footy again – I'll get back to that shortly – I also accepted a few amateur fights here and there. There were two main exhibition bouts: one with Foster Bibron and another with a Polish heavyweight. Bibron, who was born in Hawthorn, finished his professional career with 27 wins from 41 fights and a 37% KO rate. I didn't mind going rounds with these types of blokes, I'd often earn three pounds for sparring.

It got to a point where Hilton would arrange workouts with more well-known boxers at the time such as Pran Mikus, Luigi Coluzzi, Ricardo Marcos and Colin Clarke. These were serious fucking fighters. One of the toughest workouts I ever had was with South African boxer, Mike Holt, who was ranked No. 2 in the world at the time.

After returning home from a fight in Tasmania with a pair of cut eyebrows and eyes that looked like raccoons, my future wife, understandably, told me it was her or the fighting. That ended my time in the ring rather abruptly.

While all this was happening, I did make my return to the football field with Port Melbourne (Colts and Amateurs). I played with both sides from 1957-59 and added a few more games with the Colts in 1960.

But diving back into 1955 and the Montague Rovers, the Sunday League specialists were the last team I played for as an underage against the older boys. Arthur 'Kicka' Martini coached for the two seasons I was there, and it was his job to prepare us for the physical beating we were lined up to receive every week. Some people went to Sunday mass every weekend; I received my spiritual awakening on the footy field.

Made up largely of bikies, boxers, gangsters and disenchanted ex-VFL thugs, the Sunday League was the toughest footy I ever played. Winning the footy in the contest was one thing, but being able to wear the countless hits was another.

While the physical beatings, fist fights and threats of gun violence were a weekly occurrence, so too was the consistently high standard of play. It was seriously good footy. Crowds flocked to the grounds every Sunday to witness the actual game, with the sideshow of left hooks and kicks to the face also worth the price of admission. We didn't win a flag during my time with Montague, but it was certainly a solid foundation for any young man about to embark on life's journey.

On Saturday afternoons, a group of us young blokes would knock around at the Ross Street Milk Bar in Port Melbourne and play half-structured games of cricket and footy.

During the week before Christmas in 1956, a car pulled up next to our game of paper footy (I could still kick the thing over a wheat silo) and a burly man with a crew cut stepped out. Joey 'Sheepshead' Harrison was his name, and he had stopped by to recruit us to the Port Melbourne Amateurs – the VAFA club he coached. They played in E Grade Amateurs and they were short of players. A group of us took Joey up on his offer to attend training and it turned out to be one of the best decisions we could have made at that time in our lives.

Joey was incredibly talented at creating a relaxed and enjoyable atmosphere where the love of playing footy with your mates was the most important thing. And if his jokes ever fell flat or went over our too-young-to-fully-understand-your-quality-comedy heads, he always got a few laughs with his thick, ultra-Australian and at times hard-to-understand slang.

FOOTY THE GREAT LEVELLER

Fuck me dead, I've been flat out like a lizard drinking.

Fair dinkum, it's hard yakka coaching you bunch of galahs.

He was an unusual bloke, but he was down to earth and created a great sense of team spirit and comradery. In no time, we accomplished incredible success with two consecutive premierships in E Section (1957) and D Section (1958).

PORT MELBOURNE AMATEURS (1957)

The football club was going places under Joey and Robbie McPhee. That was until disaster struck on our end-of-year football trip to Warrnambool and Joey was killed in a car accident. It was heartbreaking. The man who had pulled us all together was gone in the blink of an eye.

His death broke the club. The Administration fell to pieces and the on-field performances turned to shit. It was soon thereafter that the VAFA expelled Port Amateurs from the competition for repeated violence from players and fans.

In hindsight, of course they deserved to be removed. But as one looks back on life, they ask themselves what could have been for that club. Had Joey's tragedy never occurred, would their fate have been different? Would we have stayed around? Given they were expelled one year after we won that second flag, I would assume things would have been very different.

While all of this was happening, I was simultaneously plying my trade at Port Melbourne Colts. I have purposely left the Colts until last because of the importance the club holds in my heart and the significance it had on my own coaching career. After all the years I played and coached, never could I thank a club more for giving me so much. And I owe it all to Brian 'Moppa' McBroom.

Moppa was a father figure to me. Far more than my own father and any other male 'leader' in my life. He was the greatest individual and most remarkable coach I've met. If he had decided to test his coaching skills at VFL level, I've no doubt he would've had incredible success. His knowledge of the game was second-to-none and his foresight of how it should be played was before its time.

His planning was meticulous, and he believed in a tough and unrelenting game style that came under the umbrella of 'acute discipline'.

His modus operandi was basic: win the ball at every contest, make no mistakes, kick long to the danger zones, and for fuck's sake, do not overuse the handball. He taught us to understand our teammates' strengths and weaknesses and encouraged us to show courage. Always. Despite coaching in the 1950s, Moppa would constantly rotate the rucks and onballers with half forwards and pockets. He was a marvel.

In his playing days, Moppa was a VFA state representative with Port Melbourne. He was signed by South Melbourne in the VFL, but injury cut down his career. While coaching us, he would often sit on the bench when we were short of players and if trouble struck, he would bring himself on and turn the game in our favour. He was taking the piss.

During my own coaching career, I answered many phone calls from Moppa when we were on a losing streak, and he would dissect my game plan from top to bottom as he tried to find (and fix) the issue.

Moppa passed away in 1994 at the age of just 58 but he will always hold a special place in my heart. What a brain and what a human being. He would always trouble the comfortable and, just as importantly, comfort the troubled.

I often think of how he received his nickname and how apt it was. According to his aunt and cousin, a young Moppa would threaten anyone who crossed him by finishing with *"....and then I'll mop the floor with you."* What a man and what an influence on the early stages of my career.

As you can see, the early stages of my football career helped shape me as a player and as a coach. I would take these lessons with me throughout life because there's no doubt, I was required to comfort the troubled. A lot.

TAKING SCREAMERS AT KILSYTH (1962)

IT'S 500 UP FOR A 'SEMI-INVALID'

Written by Caroline Wilson

In 1955, Laurie Aghan was told he would not walk properly again.

The Port Melbourne boy was just 17, grossly overweight and suffering acute rheumatic carditis.

"I looked like Genghis Khan – I'd spent the whole year in Prince Henry's Hospital and I weighed about 17 stone (108kg)," he said.

"But when they told me I was going to be a semi-invalid, I just couldn't accept it."

Disobeying doctor's orders, Laurie began running daily along the local beach. He stopped taking the cortisone which had increased his weight and in 12 months he lost 32kg.

In 1956 he joined amateur football club Port Melbourne, where he played 40 games in two premiership teams in as many years.

When his current team, Old Melburnians, meet St. Bernard's tomorrow, Laurie will celebrate his 500th game in amateur football.

"To be honest, I was never a great player. I've never molded myself on anyone, but really I'm a poor man's Ron Barassi," he said.

"A few weeks ago, I decided to sit down and see just how many games I'd coached.

"I worked out I'd coached 750 open age games and almost 460 with the amateurs – with 40 games as a player that makes it 500 tomorrow.

"All I could think of was, 'Jeez, my wife hasn't seen much of me over the years'."

The record of present day VFL coaches pales beside Aghan's. He has seen his amateur teams win nine premierships and run second seven times.

The Old Scotch Collegians, where he coached for six years, won the B Grade flag in 1977 and did the same in A Grade the following year.

"After coaching a side like Reservoir, I think they wondered how I'd cope with a public school like Scotch – they needed a Port Melbourne guy like me to toughen them up.

"The first day I went there, Scotch held a barbeque so all the players could meet the new coach. About four people turned up.

"As we left, my wife asked, 'What are we doing here?' and I said, 'Look at them, don't they need me?'"

Aghan coached VFA side Yarraville in 1975. He has not coached in the VFL, but was asked to apply for the job of assistant coach at Melbourne in 1980, and at Collingwood in 1975.

"At Melbourne, I think I was just an afterthought – they'd already decided to give Adrian Gallagher the job," he said.

"But I think I would have changed that club a bit. I'm pretty aggressive and I'm no 'yes' man."

Former Collingwood defender Andrew Ireland, who Aghan coached in the VAFA state side in 1974, told Aghan he would have made the grade with ease.

"I've always barracked for the Swans. I even offered them my services a few years back, but they turned me down," he said.

"I think I would have been an instant success in the VFL, but I'm 44 now so it's probably too late," he said.

"But I think the Amateurs' win against the VFA this year proves there's not a competition outside the VFL as good as the VAFA.

"As far as untapped potential goes, the amateurs are incredible. Some of the guys here would walk into a VFL side- our captain Rohan Brown for one.

"The best football player I've ever seen never play in the VFL. Ross Duke, who captained Parade and came to Scotch as my assistant."

7

VFL MISSES

> 'Victory is in having done your best.
> If you've done your best, you've won.'
> **BILL BOWERMAN, FORMER U.S. TRACK AND FIELD COACH.**

SINCE I RETIRED FROM coaching in 2001, I've reflected on my career and the incredible journey it's taken me on. The highs, the lows, and the what ifs.

Would I have been able to save the great Reservoir Old Boys from disbanding if I had stayed a few seasons longer?

Would Scotch have earned one or maybe two more senior premierships in the early 80s?

Would I have been a successful VFL coach if given the opportunity?

We'll never know the answers to these questions and I'm certainly not the person to ask. Nevertheless, I will use this chapter to reminisce about my 'near misses' at VFL level as both a player and a coach.

In January 1958, I received a letter from South Melbourne Football Club secretary, Joe White, inviting me down to training. I was coming off a successful E Grade premiership campaign for Port Melbourne Amateurs and could only assume Joe had caught wind of my talent from the myriad of groupies who watched the fifth-highest standard of footy in the VAFA.

As soon as I arrived at training and asked to speak to Joe, I knew something was wrong. He was a crusty old man and not one for light-hearted frivolities so when my name wasn't on his list, he was far from impressed.

I never sent you a letter.

I have it right here. Look, it's got the South Melbourne letterhead.

It's fake, son. Someone is taking the piss.

You are fucking kidding me!? To say I was embarrassed would be an understatement. I instantly knew it had to be one of two blokes: Reggie Smyth or Bobby Byrnes. Those two were as thick as thieves and that sort of practical joke was right in their wheelhouse.

Before I could reach into my bag of adjectives to describe how I felt about the stitch up, Joe asked for my age and playing history before he invited me to train anyway. I was as fit as I had ever been and trained the house down. Despite only going down to training because of a fake letter, I made every post a winner during that session. Joe, who was clearly impressed with what he saw, asked me to continue training with the club.

I was selected in South's first practice match against St Kilda and found myself rucking against reigning Brownlow Medallist, Brian Gleeson. Just as I had made my boxing debut against Kenny Boyd, I was now entering the most important game of life against the guy who had just been ranked the number one player in the VFL.

> Brian Gleeson's football career took him from the heights of ecstasy to the depths of despair within the space of a few short months. In 1957, his fifth season in the VFL, he produced displays of consistent all-round brilliance throughout the year to end up as an emphatic winner of both the Brownlow Medal and the St Kilda club champion award. He also played four outstanding games for the VFL that year. – John Devaney.

The game ended abruptly and in devastating fashion for Brian. Early in the first quarter as we jostled for front position at a boundary throw-in, the athlete of the two came over the top of me and landed awkwardly on his knee. That injury not only ended his day, but ultimately forced Brian into early retirement at the age of 23. The poor bastard didn't play another League game.

> In 1958, St Kilda appointed the twenty-three-year-old Gleeson as club captain, but in a pre-season practice match he injured a knee and never played VFL football again. Had he been able to continue, it is at least arguable that he would have developed into one of football's all-time greats as he was one of those rare players who appeared to have all the skills of the game at his disposal.
>
> A superb aerialist, he began his career as a strong marking centre half forward before developing into a first-rate ruckman whose ability to direct his hit-outs to his rovers was second to none. Where he outshone

> most opposition ruckmen, however, was in his extraordinary, rover-like ability on the ground; small wonder the umpires latched onto him with such unanimity in his Brownlow year.

I committed fully to training and gave it everything I had. Unfortunately, I was unable to survive the list cull and was placed on the emergency list. I returned to Port Amateurs for the 1958 season and featured in a second consecutive premiership – a 22-point victory over Bellfield.

In later years, the truth of the Joe White letter came out as the handywork of Bobby Byrnes and Trevor Castlehow. The joke was on them though after that pre-season turned out to be one of the great experiences of my playing career. I met Joe White, Crackers Goldsmith, and Billy Gunn. Not bad for a shit gag.

Fast-forward to 1975 and my next 'brush' with the VFL occurred when I was taking part in group training sessions with Collingwood's trainer, Harry King. Harry ran the sessions mainly for office workers but because it was at Victoria Park, it included Pies committeemen David Galbally, Tom Sherrin, and Bill Twomey.

While doing my best Peter Norman impression around Victoria Park one afternoon, Bill pulled me aside for a brief discussion about amateur football. He asked about our win over South Australia in 1974 and he was particularly interested in the rise of Reservoir. That discussion turned into a follow-up meeting with Bill and Tom one week later where the two of them detailed the vacant Collingwood job. Collingwood? Really? Is this another joke? I thought the approach was a bit over the top, but by the same token I was more than happy to throw my hat in the ring. I mean shit, it was Collingwood Football Club.

Unfortunately, the out-of-nowhere dream position went to one of the club's favourite sons and premiership player, Murray Weideman. If I'm going to miss out on a coaching opportunity for the black and white army, it might as well be a three-time Copeland Trophy winner and AFL Hall of Fame member.

Four years later while I was coaching at Old Scotch, I received a phone call from Ray Manley. He asked me to interview for an assistant coaching role at Melbourne Football Club under Carl Ditterich. At that point, I had experienced success with Reservoir, the state side and now Old Scotch, having taken them to the A Grade premiership in 1978. You always think you're better than you are, and I was a hot ticket.

I agreed to meet with the Melbourne hierarchy. One of the members of the group was Demons legend Hassa Mann. For those unaware of Hassa's accolades, he was a three-time premiership player, a three-time Keith 'Bluey' Truscott Medallist and a big-headed prick. During the interview, he was the one who grilled me about strategy and playing patterns. In retrospect, this is where it all fell apart.

Carl has a system and pattern of play that he will implement. You'll be required to employ that system.

You need to think though Hassa, will the same pattern of play hold up on a windy day, a sunny day, and a wet day?

We firmly believe it will. So that's what will happen.

Well, you lot must be morons.

The meeting didn't last much longer. Apparently calling the selection panel a pack of buffoons wasn't the done thing. When

I arrived home, I gave Lorna a ten-minute sermon about how I'd just met the world's greatest arsehole.

How wrong I was. In later years, I got to know Hassa and his wife Glenys through our shared social group. If you don't know the man – which I certainly didn't during the interview – you can easily form the opinion that he's up himself. He's direct, he's professional, and he's a perfectionist. Not exactly the worst combination of traits.

Our friendship has come the full 180° over the past few years. We've morphed into the ultimate odd couple. We speak every week, and we travel together on family holidays. I was lucky enough to attend his AFL Hall of Fame Induction in 2013 and share that special moment with him and his family. He's a champion in all respects and that's why I was honoured to hear he would contribute to the Forward in this book.

Would I have been a successful VFL coach? Maybe not. But I really don't know. What I do know is that these 'near-misses' were achievements in themselves. My hard work was rewarded by being a part of the conversation and I have always been proud of that. And while I may not have joined Collingwood or even Melbourne as an assistant coach, what it did bring me was one of the greatest mates a man could ask for. That's a win.

8

RESERVOIR OLD BOYS
(1970 – 1974)

> 'Treat a person as he is, and he will remain as he is. Treat him as he could be, and he will become what he should be.'
> **JIMMY JOHNSON, TWO-TIME SUPER BOWL CHAMPION.**

GOOD BUT NOT GOOD enough. That was the story of my playing career. I created great memories with the likes of Port Amateurs, Colts, Northcote (VFA), Kilsyth, and Sandringham (VFA), but my knowledge of the game meant I knew from a young age that I would never achieve all I wanted as a player. Coaching was always going to be my ticket to success.

After breaking my leg at East Malvern Amateurs in 1969 and ending my career with a trip to Prince Henry Hospital in the back of a ute tray, my playing days were over. It had been 18 years and 372 games on the field with two premierships at Port Melbourne Amateurs and another at Northcote. Representing the VFA against the Ferntree Gully League while running around in the Sandringham stripes was certainly a highlight, but nothing compared to the celebrations of the Northcote flag. 103 games for the Brickfielders and not once did I pull up as sore as I did on that Sunday morning.

I had already completed a season as captain-coach at Kilsyth eight years earlier and began to seriously consider my options on the coaching frontier. Lorna and I were living in Preston with Kimmy and Jason at the time, and I was approached by Lorna's godson and Reservoir Old Boy's senior captain, Laurie McLaughlin, about his side's vacant senior coaching role in the Victorian Amateur Football Association (VAFA).

Laurie, I know you haven't coached for a while, but we've stagnated. We need someone to take us to the next level.

I'm certainly interested. But I'll need to meet the committee and make sure we're on the same page.

Reservoir formed five seasons earlier in 1965 and they had experienced instant success with an F Grade premiership against Old Ivanhoe Grammarians. However, they had failed to capitalise on the momentum of their inaugural season and still lingered in E Grade four years later.

After advising Laurie Mac that I was interested in putting my hand up for the role, he organised a meeting at Gary Veith's home with Fred Tuininga, John Buckley, Gary, and himself. At the meeting, Fred quickly established himself as the unofficial Head of the Coaching Recruitment Team and flexed his muscle with a lot of questions about my previous experience.

FOOTY THE GREAT LEVELLER

So why do you think you failed at Kilsyth?

Jesus, I wouldn't call it a failure.

You weren't reappointed after one year, correct?

Correct. But the President was a dickhead.

Fred was a reliable centre-half back and future captain of the club, having migrated from Holland with his parents. While we would eventually form an incredible friendship, at that initial meeting I didn't have the highest opinion of him. To say the least.

Why I hadn't been reappointed at Kilsyth and my record wasn't too flash, it was a record I knew I could improve at an E Grade amateur club. I asked my own questions of the group and learnt that, while they had experienced success a few years earlier under Barry Evans, they had gone been treading water since. They simply wanted to solidify their position under new leadership in the upcoming season and build from there. There was certainly no expectation to rise from the ashes of E Section to the heights of A in consecutive years. There was no greater example of the committee's bleak outlook than the $200 annual salary I was offered to coach both seniors and reserves. Fortunately, I never coached for the money, which is just as well because that number didn't change in five seasons.

The group explained the club had a solid feeder program with Reservoir High School and if those ties continued to be strengthened, they could attract serious young talent instead of losing out to local rivals offering match payments. I also learnt that a lot of Reservoir players lived in commission housing and required a great deal of discipline and guidance. As someone who could relate to a rougher-than-your-average upbringing, this was the challenge and the role for me. I received a phone call from Laurie Mac one week after that meeting confirming my appointment as coach of the seniors and reserves, and the next phase of my football career had begun.

I was impressed with the first training session in late 1969, with 30 players attending and a reasonable level of ability on show. In a bid to attract more talent from Reservoir High, Freddie, Johnny 'Spidge' Martin, Laurie Mac and I decided to host a Pie Night and marketed the event with flyers around the school. Rentokil sponsored the night with 60 pies and pasties, but it soon became obvious that wasn't nearly enough. We were training at the school on the evening of the Pie Night when a large group of teenagers with schoolbags started jumping over the wire fencing surrounding the ground. It caused quite the stir with about 20 of them arriving together.

What do you want boys?

There's a Pie Night here isn't there?

Yes, there certainly is.

Oh well, I guess we're here to play footy then.

Just like that, the club had attracted another team's worth of recruits and the $200 salary was quickly re-invested in additional pies. Reservoir had 37 players on the list in 1969 and suddenly we had 57. I fucking love those meat pies.

There were a small group of players who initially stood out; Graham 'Fatty' Carr, Paul Brooks, and Allan Dunn. Not so much for their talent, but because they were heart and soulers. Fatty and Brooksy epitomised team spirit as they happily completed any task asked of them. Whether it was cutting oranges, running the boundary or organising social events, those two did what was required. Dunn, on the other hand, was popular among his teammates because he was a knockaround kid who could handle himself in almost any altercation. Of course, that wasn't the case when he took exception to my training methods one evening and tried to punch me. Never one to back down from a fight, I grabbed his swinging hand, pulled him closer to me and smacked him across the chin. It was flush. After that incident, Dunny's attitude completely changed. Thank fuck, I was getting too old to be throwing perfectly timed jabs.

Training went up a gear as we focused on both the physical and mental aspect of the game. While we would only be competing in the fifth highest section of the amateurs (or second lowest if your glass is half empty), I was a disciplinarian from the outset and based my coaching philosophies on learnings I took from Moppa McBroom; discipline, a positive attitude towards training and direct play.

Physically, Reservoir had few issues. Popular lingo from opposition clubs over the next few years would centre around our no-nonsense approach to the game – *'unfashionable'*, *'hard-nosed'*, *'dirty fucking bastards'* - that sort of thing. The boys were simply contested beasts. If I said, *'go and hit someone'*, they wouldn't think twice about it. But it was their appetite for the contest and their unrivalled comradery that set them apart.

It was clear the group had grown up together because their ability to learn each other's strengths and weaknesses was instant. I wanted them to know who the strongest kicks were, who the highest marks were, and who the hardest players were. Equally, I wanted them to know who struggled in those aspects of the game. My main objective was to strengthen our strengths and eliminate our weaknesses. Everyone bought into it. Players who couldn't handball or kick on their opposite side would practice those skills, players who weren't as fit would run extra 440s, players who skirted the packs would improve their contested play. Ultimately, that's how we won. We got to understand each other's game perfectly.

After a string of impressive pre-season matches, Round 1 was a minor disappointment when we opened the season with a five-point loss to Brunswick. In his weekly column in 'The Amateur Footballer', George McTaggart noted it was the only E Section match with any competitiveness in the opening round and, as it turned out, would act as a precursor to the grand final. The seniors officially entered the winner's column the following week with a commanding 67-point win over State Savings Bank and kick-started a fantastic run of victories. We finished the home and away season in second spot with a 16-2 record. We came together unbelievably as a football side. Halfway through the season, I thought there was something here, there's something in this place.

Our finals chances took a massive and soul-sucking hit in Round 17 when our ruckman, Michael Bates, received a four-match suspension for striking an Elsternwick player. It was the worst-case scenario – even if we lost the second semi and had to play every match ahead of the grand final, he still wouldn't have been available for selection until Round 1 the following year. Fuck.

Michael Bates is second to only Ross Duke (Old Paradians) as the most gifted player I've coached during my VAFA career. He was a first-class ruckman with an unrivalled ability to take the game away from the opposition. Batesy was a double threat. He had an abundance of God-given natural talent, but he also embraced the fitness component of the game and boasted an aerobic capacity that put the more vertically challenged onballers to shame. At one pre-season camp in Portsea, he threw me on his shoulders (at almost 14 stone) and carried me up a 100-foot sand dune. He hardly broke a sweat. Animal. Batesy's only issue was that if he felt shithouse and didn't want to play, he couldn't be inspired to lift.

I'm done for the day.

Mate, I need another 20 minutes from you.

Nah, I'm fucking done.

They were isolated incidents but when he didn't want to be there, he couldn't be persuaded to lift, and it often cost us the game. I've no doubt it cost him a VFL career.

After my first season with Reservoir, Batesy joined Essendon (1971) and managed two games in the reserves before returning to amateur football. It was a huge positive for us as he won the 1975 Woodrow Medal as the A Grade best & fairest and played a leading hand in our premierships at both Reservoir and Old Scotch. Geez, I loved that man.

Despite the disappointment of Batesy's suspension, we had great depth in our squad. This was no more evident than the fact the reserves finished on top of the ladder with 17 wins and 242.8%. They were dominant. They had just 557 points kicked against them for the season, which was the lowest of any section in the Association. Unfortunately, the winning form for both sides failed to hold up in finals, with the seniors falling to Brunswick by 21 in the decider, and the reserves getting handed a 44-point belting by Elsternwick. Ross Letson, Geoff Trevascus, and Johnny Martin were outstanding for us against Brunswick, but we had no way of filling our Michael Bates-sized canyon in the middle of the ground and countering the aerial dominance of their ruckman.

> Brunswick led Reservoir Old Boys all day and won by 21 points, the high marking of both sides being a feature of the game. The Reservoir rovers were on top but Brunswick won across the centre and their rucks took charge in the second half. The game was very even with Brunswick leading by 10 points at half-time. Their more accurate attack could have been a big factor in their win.
>
> George McTaggart.

Irrespective of the result, we had earnt promotion to D Section for the first time in the club's short history. We were building something special, and everyone could feel it.

The success of promotion led to the greatest influx of talent in my five years at the helm. Terry Archer, Danny McGaw, Garry Massey, Jimmy Paulka, Howard Devlin, Danny Barclay, and Kevin McCrohan all joined ahead of my second year. Suddenly, we were the front runners.

We lost just one game during the home and away season and reached the grand final with a 13-point win over Brunswick – who we fucking hated by that stage - in the second semi-final. The fourth-ranked Power House found another gear in the finals and defeated both Parkside and the vegetarians in consecutive matches to set up a 1 v 4 grand final showdown. With Brunswick out of the picture, the game was ours to lose. Well, until the fourth quarter. Leading by nine points at three-quarter time, we were absolutely belted in the final term as Peter Hutchinson led Power House to seven goals and the win. Hutchy was clearly the difference. Had Batesy not been at Essendon, it would have been a different story. It was a 15-point loss in the end, but it might as well have been 150. Two straight grand final losses and promotion to a higher section again.

Ahead of the 1972 C Section season, we acquired more talent in the form of Wayne Ayres, Tommy Byrne, Alan and Ray Shepherd. A quiet and talented 17-year-old kid, Ray quickly established himself as the fittest player to wear a Reservoir jumper. He was a running machine, often overlapping teammates at training while completing my infamous 440s. Most of the players hated my 440s. Not Ray. That kid was the terminator. More than anything, his elite endurance gave us another weapon as we looked to end a frustrating run of grand final losses.

The addition of Ray was an important victory for the club against local rivals and indicative of the young talent we were attracting after two seasons of improved results. That year, he joined Jimmy Paulka (20), Danny McGaw (20), Terry Archer (19), Gary Massey (20), Howard Devlin (20), and Tommy Byrne (21) – all talented young men who would have sat comfortably in any A Grade side.

There was great optimism as we entered the season and that only grew once we'd dismantled the best Diamond Valley teams during practice games. We didn't slow down from there either. After claiming an 85-point Round 1 victory over Fairfield, we never looked back.

No team came close to us during the home and away season as we won 18 consecutive matches with an average score of 144. Four of our players – McCrohan (64), Martin (52), Archer (42) and Ayres (41) - finished in the top 10 goal kickers for C Section. Just as impressively, we didn't have a single player poll more than 12 votes in the VAFA best and fairest award. We had an even spread of contributors and they were all fucking good.

Coming up against Assumption in the grand final, it was clearly our best chance yet to achieve premiership success. It was our best chance to do what we had failed to do over the previous two years. We were in form, and we hadn't given them a sniff all season with three wins by an average of 37 points. It certainly wasn't a done deal though. They had this old-timer running around by the name of Des Tuck. And he was an enormous threat.

Des was a Marist Brother at Marcellin College and had only recently debuted in the VAFA after the Brothers relaxed rules that prohibited competitive sport outside of school. His brother, Frank, played 131 games for Collingwood, including two years as captain in the late 50s. Had Des decided against joining the Marist Brothers when he was 13 years old, there is no doubt he too would have played VFL football. Or Test cricket. Or tennis. Or professional golf. He could probably swim as well. Despite being unable to play since the age of 16, Des had returned 14 years later and had not skipped a beat. He slotted 92 goals and finished second in the competition best and fairest count at the age of 30. He was a 6'4" centre-half forward and the one player I knew could deny us that elusive premiership.

With Batesy the only member of our entire grand final team as tall as Tuck, the job was given to Danny McGaw. Danny was behind only Batesy and Kevin Grose as the most talented players I coached at Reservoir and should have played league footy. While there were players at the club who never needed motivation to train, Danny certainly wasn't in that category. He was the life of the party, always laughing and refusing to take anything too seriously. He would either have me in fits of laughter or frustration. There was no in between.

When tasked with negating Tuck, Danny did take it seriously. Very seriously. He kept the Brother to three goals for the match and played a leading hand in our emphatic 46-point victory. It was one of the best performances I had seen.

With scores level at 14-14 at quarter time, we won the game in the second term with 10 goals to one. What a feeling to watch Howard Devlin in full flight as he kicked a game-high six goals. To see the maturity of Michael Bates as he controlled the ruck contest on the biggest stage. Or Ray Shepherd producing a remarkable performance as the youngest player on the ground.

> After an even first quarter, Reservoir Old Boys raced away from Assumption in the second term when they added 10-4 to 1-1, and were more than 9 goals in front at the interval. They went further ahead in the third quarter and although Assumption did better in the last, Reservoir ran out easy winners by 46 points, to go through the season undefeated.
>
> George McTaggart.

The reserves had broken their own grand final hoodoo earlier in the day and defeated St Kilda CBOC, giving Reservoir the seniors-reserves C Section double. What a feeling. As one would imagine, the celebrations were insane, starting at the clubrooms and Gary Veith's home before venturing to Preston Town Hall on Mad Monday. The world was our oyster. We had been promoted three years in a row and we'd now won a flag as a champion team. It was just the fifth undefeated season in C Grade history. We were heading up to B Grade full of confidence.

As we climbed through the grades, the club continued to improve each year via internal maturation and the addition of new recruits. During the 1973 off-season, we added a player who exemplified the traditional Reservoir way of life. Without question, Kevin Grose was the best junior footballer I have ever seen. When he arrived as a 19-year-old ahead of our journey into the unchartered waters of B Grade, we went from a finals fancy to unbackable favouritism. He was quick, he was strong, he kicked goals, and his unrelenting attack on the ball was second to absolutely nobody. Pure and simple, he was one of the greatest movers I have ever seen in my life. And there was no chance you could miss him. He was inked to the nines, with artwork in the Kevin Murray and Robert McGhie mould. Or Dane Swan for the younger ones playing at home.

Grosey played a couple of seasons for Reservoir OB before he was picked up by Collingwood. This included a best-on-ground performance in the 1974 Big V match against South Australia. In fact, it was the Big V match that officially caught the attention of Magpies recruiters, with Grosey kicking three goals in the second half and helping us to a rare win against the Croweaters. He was named on the half-forward flank in the All-Australian Amateur team and had it all before him.

He managed 32 games for Collingwood from 1975-77 but could have notched 300 if he could have played the game. Not the game of footy, but the professional game. As a red-blooded Reservoir boy, Grosey was too often found drinking piss with his mates at the Summerhill Hotel. When he was selected by the Magpies, he couldn't break away from that environment. He couldn't say, *'I'm going to be a league footballer'*. Instead, it was, *'I'm a Reservoir boy, I want to drink with my mates, and fuck ya I will still play league footy'*. Unfortunately, that attitude didn't fly with the suits and three years after debuting, he was leading North Heidelberg in the Diamond Valley Football League. There are many great stories about Grosey, but there is no better example of his love for his mates than when he won $200 as Collingwood's 'Player of the Month' in 1976 and spent it on a party for his teammates. That was him to a tee. A great man.

With Grosey entering the fold in 1973, we steamrolled our way through B Grade. 14 wins, three losses and one draw (against Brian Steele's Old Carey) we finished two and a half games clear at the top of the ladder. There was a distinct difference to that finals series from the previous three, however, because now we were playing for promotion to A Grade. We were playing for a chance to take on the VAFA's best.

There's a line regularly used in amateur football that *'promotion is for the club while a premiership is for the coach and his players'*. I can tell you, with a spot in A Grade up for grabs, I fucking wanted both. Heading into the second semi-final against University Blacks, we were quietly confident. We'd already beaten them twice throughout the year by 31 and 25, respectively. After an inaccurate first term where we kicked 1.7 and trailed by eight points, the semi played out exactly as I had hoped, and we ran away with a 47-point victory. Again, we did ourselves no favours in front of goal with 11.22 (88), but when the opposition is held to just 39 points for the match, the defenders deserve a beer or two.

Having earned a spot in the VAFA's top section after languishing in E Grade just three years earlier, the confidence was at an all-time high. We were walking in rare air and only had one more job to do to cement our place in history. Two weeks later, we inked the Reservoir name in the books by claiming the B Grade flag with a 21-point win over the Blacks. While they had names like Costello and Cordner running around, the game was all but over by quarter time after we piled on 9.6 (60) to 2.0 (12) in one of the most explosive 25 minutes of football

I'd witnessed. It was one of the most memorable days of my life. A Grade and a flag. It doesn't get any better.

RESERVOIR SENIORS B GRADE PREMIERS (1973)

Despite the success of that 1973 season, it wasn't all smooth sailing. Entering A Grade in 1974 brought about the first signs of uneasiness at the club. It should have been the most exciting pre-season of them all, but a handful of player departures rapidly brought us back down to earth. It was no longer enough to '*treat him as he could be*' when Diamond Valley clubs were offering players $300-$400 per game. How could we compete with that?

While a few fringe players had taken the money, it was only when Ray Shephard was poached that I thought we were fucked. Add in a season-ending injury to Batesy in Round 5 and another to McCrohan in Round 10, and that level of fucked turned into genuinely fucked very quickly. We were pushing shit up an A Grade hill. We managed seven wins and finished in seventh spot on the ladder, but we were no match for Ormond, Coburg, or St Bernard's. These teams were genuine powerhouses of the competition, and we lacked three to four quality players. Our

B Grade side would've won A Grade standing on our heads, but the loss of personnel prior to and during the season stamped our papers. We somehow managed to win the reserves flag that season so it wasn't all doom and gloom. But it certainly was the same level of celebration as 12 months earlier.

That's where things really began to turn. Arguments started at committee level and filtered into the playing group. Even Freddie started questioning me.

> *What don't you change our game plan?*

> *It's got nothing to do with the game plan, Fred. No footy side would survive the amount of talent we've lost. None.*

As it turned out, it didn't survive for much longer.

After five seasons, I felt the club needed a fresh voice. I had taken Reservoir from a struggling E Grade outfit to the highest and most competitive section in the VAFA. We had won two senior and two reserves premierships and introduced the world to an incredibly talented group of young men. I was OK with that.

Looking back now, leaving the club at the end of the 1974 season was the worst decision I have ever made. They hit several stumbling blocks that I feel I could've helped prevent and they eventually folded on the eve of the 1978 season. I felt ashamed. I know if I had stayed, we would have retained the backbone of the playing list and rebuilt.

> In 1975 there was a concern that if the club should be defeated in an important A Section match its supporters might riot. At about that time it was noted that the Reservoir Old Boys' file was thicker after ten years in

the association than the Collegians' file after more than eighty years. The club was lucky not to be expelled after a 1975 finals match against North Old Boys, escaping with a $200 fine; eventually it ran into administrative and financial difficulties and withdrew before the start of the 1978 season - For the Love of the Game, The Centenary History of the Victorian Amateur Football Association, 1892-1992.

A FINAL WORD ON RESERVOIR

An important era ended when the association between Reservoir Old Boys and amateur football ended. Because of the environment and issues that existed within the club, it was evident that it was doomed. I take some responsibility for its downfall because I left in their time of need and could have provided the discipline and guidance required to successfully rebuild.

I blame the club for the numerous spectator incidents, and I blame the VAFA for its overexaggerated response to trivial incidents.

An exodus of players and officials to the Diamond Valley competition was the final nail in the Reservoir coffin; a club with one of the most storied 13-year histories in Australian rules football.

Let us remember this once great club for its finals successes, its competition best and fairest winners, and for its interstate representatives.

I believe Reservoir tried to their utmost to comply with the association's rules and, instead of the memories of their off-field notoriety, believe they should be remembered for their on-field excellence.

I am indebted to many people at the club, but offer special thanks to Graham 'Fatty' Carr, Neil Macklin, Billy and Tommy Byrne, Jimmy and Kevin Paulka, and Geoff Trevascus for the organisation and success of the past three reunions. I know this club will continue to be remembered.

One of its stars, Gary Massey, told me that without the Old Boys he would have achieved nothing.

Treat a person as he is, and he will remain as he is. Treat him as he could be, and he will become what he should be.

Who would have thought that in five seasons from 1970-1974, Reservoir Old Boys would have reached the heights of A Grade football? Who would have predicted a B and C Grade premiership?

My sincere thanks to everyone at Reservoir. You gave me so much and you will all be in my heart while I am on this planet.

RESERVOIR RESERVES (1973)

9

OLD SCOTCH COLLEGIANS

(1975 – 1981, 1988 & 1990)

> 'Winners are grinners, and losers can please themselves.'
> **TEDDY WHITTEN, FOOTSCRAY CHAMPION.**

WHEN I WAS APPOINTED as state coach in 1974 and led the Amateurs to victory against South Australia, it was the second time I had met Scotch captain and star midfielder, John Anderson.

I had previously met Ando during the 1973 B Section Grand Final against University Blacks. It was a tough game that we eventually won 17.12 (114) to 15.3 (93), but Ando decided to introduce himself at the half-time break. Reservoir had just given up six goals to three in the second term after leading by 46 points at the first break. While I was trying to figure out reasons for the drop-off in intensity, this immaculately dressed man with a perfectly sculptured jawline and socks with his initials (JA) emblazoned on them, had the audacity to pick that exact moment to speak to me.

Hi coach, do you think we'll win?

Yes, I do actually.

Excellent. I'm John Anderson by the way, captain of Old Scotch.

Nice to meet you, John. Do you mind if I address my players now?

My confidence in the result was not quite as high when Uni Blacks slotted another five goals to one and trailed by just six points at three-quarter time, but we managed to kick away in the final term. Thank fuck.

When Ando and I first interacted in 1973, he had already established himself as one of the champions of Old Scotch. He was recruited from Scotch College in 1966 and debuted in the seniors in his first year. He had already won three of his six club best & fairest awards (1969, 1970, 1972, 1974, 1976 & 1977) and had played in the two previous representative programs.

By the time he retired in 1980, Ando had carved one of the greatest Amateur careers on record. 229 club games, three premierships (two as captain) and six years in the state team. My relationship with him as coach and captain was of the utmost importance to me, and it was one of the proudest days of my life when we were named in those positions on the OSCFC Team of the 20th Century.

Ando was a unique individual and if there's one thing I quickly learnt, he always had an agenda. After our initial contact at the B Section Grand Final and the South Australia game, Ando attended a couple of Yarraville matches during my one-year stint in 1975.

It was not long thereafter I received a phone call from him asking if I'd be interested in coaching Old Scotch. The seniors had won the B Section premiership in 1970 but were relegated one year later with just three wins. They had been battling aimlessly in B Grade since and were hellbent on achieving the ultimate success in A Grade. It was something they hadn't done since 1934. Initially, I declined Ando's offer. I was pissed off with how things ended at Yarraville and wanted a break from coaching.

Ando was unphased by my response and followed up with another phone call one week later, asking me to lunch at the Flagstaff Hotel. He knew that my craving for an A Grade premiership was as deep as his. He knew that winners were grinners and losers, well, fuck being a loser. Alright, I'm going to lunch. A man's got to eat.

When I arrived at the Flagstaff Hotel, I was surprised to see the handsome, well-dressed man with an agenda in a group with three others.

I thought this was a lunch between just you and I, John.

No mate, we're here to celebrate your appointment as coach of the footy club.

You've got to be kidding me.

The three men with Ando were club stalwarts Bryan Steele, Leigh McGregor, and Brian Gibbs - the Scotch Mafia. Leigh was the club's new president and a standout at that lunch, impressing with his sincerity and honesty. He admitted the club wanted someone different leading the charge, someone who wasn't an old boy and who could bring a unique and harder edge to the playing group. I already knew Bryan Steele from his time at Old Carey. In Round 7 of 1973, despite Reservoir being the far superior side, Carey managed to tie with us, and I have never heard the end of it since.

After three hours at the Flagstaff, my rubber arm had been twisted and I agreed to take on the role. But it had to be the same structure as Reservoir. I required total control of the football department, which included coaching both seniors and reserves. No interference. I wasn't going to put up with any shit.

In *A Centenary History of the Old Scotch Football Club 1921-2020*, Bruce Brown and Geoff McCracken detailed Scotch's perspective in regard to my appointment.

> Having had several years languishing in B Section, Leigh McGregor as incoming president saw the need to inject new life into the club.
>
> In appointing Steele's successor, the club responded to the strong recommendation of John Anderson and appointed Laurie Aghan as senior coach in 1976. Anderson had played for the state amateur side under Aghan and sensed that he would energise the club.
>
> Renowned as an 'old school' tough footballer, Aghan had played in the VFA and sought to instil physical and mental toughness in the way the club played.
>
> In 1982, after his first retirement from the club, he reflected on his introduction to the club with The Herald's Caroline Wilson (13 August 1982 p25).
>
> 'After coaching a side like Reservoir, I think they

> wondered how I'd cope with a public (APS) school like Scotch – they needed a Port Melbourne guy like me to toughen them up. The first day I went there, Scotch held a barbeque so all the players could meet the new coach. About four people turned up. As we left, my wife asked, 'What are we doing here?' and I said, 'Look at them, don't they need me?'

My understanding of Old Scotch and its list was non-existent when I first arrived, and the barbeque debacle certainly didn't instil me with confidence that this was an A Grade side. The only players who turned up were Bruce Kefford, John Morgan, Simon Tallent and John Anderson; four Scotch College alumni who became champions of the football club.

Kefford was a 6'6 lumbering ruckman whose greatest strength was his ability to understand an instruction and carry it out to the letter. Clearly, this was going to work well with my disciplined approach to the game. He was the only other player I knew prior to my appointment because I had coached him in the 1974 state game alongside Ando.

The other two, however, I didn't really know. John (Morgan) had two stints with Scotch over his 211-game career either side of a one-off season with Melbourne FC in 1973. Despite starring as a key forward in his junior days and being named at CHF in the *OSCFC Team of the 20th Century*, John became a reliable defender during my time at the club and was named on the half-back flank in both the '77 and '78 premiership sides. I heard several renditions of the time he kicked 16 goals in a game against Ivanhoe in 1970.

I couldn't care less, he's in the fucking backline.

FOOTY THE GREAT LEVELLER

Ando wrote me a list of all the players when I first arrived, and he detailed their strengths and weaknesses. His assessment of Simon was as positive as it was honest.

> *A great thinker and a great player. He will never let you down. Can try to do too much.*

Simon also ended up playing more than 200 games for Scotch (221) and his resume is littered with accolades: club captain, state representative, premiership player. As soon as I met him, I had great respect for his down-to-earth attitude, and I already knew he was going to be an invaluable asset to our A Grade mission.

Unimpressed and doubting the commitment of the playing group following the four-person shit show of a barbeque, my mood quickly changed on the first night of pre-season training. Like your future wife turning up late on the first date, my initial anger subsided when there were 40 players running around at Yarra Park. Ando was leading from the front, Tallent was hitting every target and Kefford was putting in more effort than any player. It was glorious.

My plan was to coach Scotch as I had Reservoir. That is with acute discipline and total control. For this to happen, I needed to earn the group's respect.

> *Ok boys, I want to let you know there's only one boss. It's not Ando, it's me. If I tell you to do something, you do it. I'll accept the mistake or I'll get the pat on the back. But right now, I want you to run six laps.*

The murmurs of *'what'*, *'huh'* and *'get fucked'* quickly spread throughout the group until Ando, who knew exactly what

I was about, took off running. He was every part a leader that man. And like a herd of apprehensive but otherwise committed animals, the rest of them followed suit.

We tasted immediate success in 1976, with the seniors and reserves both finishing on top of the ladder as minor premiers. Unfortunately, that's where the winning stopped. The seniors went down to Caulfield Grammarians in the second semi-final after leading by three goals at quarter time.

> Old Scotch kicked six goals in the first quarter against Caulfield, but Caulfield came back to lead by two points at half-time. The third quarter was even with Caulfield eight points up at the last change but they finished too strongly and were winners by nearly six goals.
>
> George McTaggart.

The finals series ended one week later for the seniors after going down to Marcellin by 34 points in the preliminary. A straight sets loss. We'd only lost three matches throughout the year. It was a fucking debacle.

> The Marcellin-Old Scotch game was even for the first half, but Marcellin broke away in the third quarter and their greater experience enabled them to go on to win by 34 points.
>
> George McTaggart.

Thankfully, after they too went down in the second semi, the reserves hit back with a preliminary final win against Marcellin before eventually going down to Ivanhoe in the decider. As disappointed as I was for both sides, it was obvious my plan was working. We hadn't won the flag and it was the first time

I hadn't coached a team to promotion in the VAFA. But clearly, I was doing something right and a finals appearance meant we were on the right track.

The talent coming out of the school the following year really helped take things to the next level for Old Scotch. We're talking names like Peter Sherwen, Tim Cox, Tom Mason, Paul Meadows, David Bowden, and Fergus Keil. They were my babies. They were young enough to be my sons and talented enough to take Scotch back to the promised land. Irrespective of whether we won the grand final or not, my remit was to lead Scotch to A Grade.

We won 14 games throughout the home and away season and again claimed the minor premiership. Coincidentally, we finished one spot above Reservoir on the ladder but were never destined to meet in the big one after they mirrored our performance one year earlier and fell in straight sets. We really were the team to beat that year as we headed into finals with the most points scored (96ppg) and lowest scored against (74ppg). It was ours to lose, but we weren't grinning just yet.

The second semi-final against Reservoir wasn't going to be easy after Ray Shepherd and Michael Bates had just finished first and second in the B Section best & fairest. Ray had polled 26 votes and although he was ineligible to win, Batesy received 17. Both players were incredible against us, but it mattered little as we kicked five goals to one in the first quarter and held on for a 27-point victory. The return to A Grade was complete. In two years, we ticked the first box and returned to the top section for the first time since 1971. Or, as the OSFC Centenary Book says, *'Phase One had been accomplished'*.

Reservoir were bundled out by Ivanhoe the following week in a one-pointer. History would show that to be the last real hoorah for my old club, so the feeling was certainly bittersweet.

Despite going 1-1 against Ivanhoe throughout the season, I liked our chances after the bruising preliminary that they had only narrowly survived. Thanks to my old Reservoir boys. Ivanhoe had added motivation, however, following The Amateur Footballer Record's announcement that Bill McWhinnie would hang up the boots.

> Ivanhoe's dynamic captain and coach, Bill McWhinnie, will lead the 'Hoes onto the ground at Collingwood today for the last time. It will be Bill's 227th game for the club in a career that started in 1965. And what a career it has been.
>
> He has certainly given his all and in doing so has won the club's Best and Fairest award three times, been runner-up on four occasions and represented Victoria in the 1970 Amateur Carnival in Perth. Bill was captain of Ivanhoe in 1968, '69 and '70, and has been captain and coach for the last four seasons.
>
> In 1969, the club won its last senior flag in 'B' Grade, and today, NO DOUBT, the "Little General" will be more determined than ever (if that's possible) to repeat the performance.

Fuck McWhinnie. Ivanhoe played a physical brand of football and every time we faced them, they'd try to kick the shit out of us. Understandably, they targeted players like Ando. At the start of the grand final at Victoria Park, McWhinnie met Ando for the coin toss. Instead of shaking hands, wishing him good luck, and giving him a light tap on the arse, McWhinnie called his teammates over to intimidate Ando by tucking their shoulders in and bumping him one-by-one. I should've sent the rest of the team over to fly the flag and tear those dickheads apart with the old Aghan left-right special, but Ando just laughed it off. And then he annihilated them.

Despite kicking 15 behinds in the first two quarters, we held a slender lead over Ivanhoe at the half-time break. Ando was dominating through the midfield, racking up disposals at will and giving them his own version of an arse tap. But realising the game was up for grabs, I took him aside for a quiet word.

Mate, if we kick the first goal in the third quarter, we'll break these blokes and we'll win this game.

Leave it with me, Coach.

That was all I needed to do. At first bounce of the second half, Ando won the clearance, took two bounces, and slotted a sensational goal from 50m before looking straight over at me as if to say, '*I just broke these blokes, Coach*'. Smart arse.

That goal started an avalanche for Scotch as we continued applied scoreboard pressure while keeping the Hoes to just two goals in the second half. At the final siren, we had secured a 42-point win. Phase Two had been accomplished.

OLD SCOTCH COLLEGIANS B GRADE PREMIERS (1977)

In between seasons, VAFA Secretary Jack Fullerton retired after 27 years in the role. He wasn't a well-liked man among the Amateur community because of the way he ran the competition. Jack was an old school operator and ruled the Association with an iron fist. Old Scotch champion and VAFA President, Manson Russel, despised him, while he wasn't the first name on John Dillon's Christmas card list. As for me, I didn't mind the man. I probably saw a bit of myself in the way it was his way or the highway. And the more I got to know him, the less of a prick he was.

It wasn't always sunshine and rainbows between Jack and me. During a must-win game against Uni Blacks, I overheard him barracking against us. We hadn't yet officially met but I was absolutely fucking ropable with his behaviour.

How dare you support a team as VAFA Secretary!

FOOTY THE GREAT LEVELLER

I'll do whatever the fuck I want.
You can just focus on the game.

Once he'd calmed down, Jack and his wife Norma invited Lorna and I around their house for dinner to apologise for his behaviour. As it turned out, he was a decent man that could just get a bit hot-headed. It sounded eerily familiar and wasn't exactly something I could hold against him.

With Phases One and Two complete at Old Scotch, the Mafia came to me and asked what we needed to secure an A Grade flag. Our list was strong, but I felt we still lacked one or two genuine match winners if we were going to cut it with the Big Three: North Old Boys, De La Salle and St Bernard's. They had been the dominant sides and played in the previous three A Section Grand Finals. As far as any reasonable VAFA tipster was concerned, they were the trio to beat.

We need to strengthen our list. We need Batesy and Dukey.

With my ties to Reservoir and those who had played in the 1974 state team, I was able to recruit Michael Bates and Ross Duke. Batesy arrived on the back of Reservoir's disbandment and the fact Freddie Tuininga, Johnny Martin and Tommy Byrne had already joined me at Yarra Park. He was a Woodrow Medallist by then and would undoubtedly add that match-winning element I was after.

At this point in the book, my thoughts on Batesy are well known. But I haven't yet given my opinion of Ross Duke. The best Amateur footballer I've ever seen.

I first went on record with my thoughts about Dukey when interviewed by Caroline Wilson ahead of my 500th game as a player and coach.

LAURIE AGHAN AND NICK ARMISTEAD

The best football player I've ever seen never played in the VFL. Ross Duke, who captained Parade and came to Scotch as my assistant.

Parade was in B Section at the time and hadn't won an A Grade flag since the final leg of their three-peat in 1968. Having coached Dukey in the 1974 state game, I knew he was the missing link. Alongside Batesy, they would take us to the next level. Finals became an expectation rather than a pipe dream.

As a player, Dukey was the epitome of a ball magnet. He'd get 50 kicks a game. He could read the ball off the pack and anticipate where it was going better than anyone. But the bloke could not kick. Of those 50 kicks, only 30 of them would hit a target. And that was a good day. It mattered little to me though because he'd get so many touches that he'd create more chances for our forwards than the rest of the team combined.

That year was a genuine rollercoaster. We won our first five games of the season and sat on top of the ladder before suffering a serious form slump and dropping eight of our next 12. We had fallen to fifth by Round 17 and needed a 20-goal win against Caulfield if we were going to play in the finals.

Heading into Round 18, we sat behind Uni Blues, Ivanhoe, De La Salle and North Old Boys. Having defeated the Blues one week earlier, we had found the sort of form required to dismantle the bottom-of-the-table Fields. De La and North were fixtured to play one another, so if we could pick up the percentage required, we were set to replace the loser of their game. What happened next was one of the great 'fuck me' moments in my entire career.

With 61 scoring shots to 25, we ran riot against Caulfield and won the game by 156 points. Tom Mason (9) and Paul Meadows (8) were unstoppable in the forward half and spearheaded quarter-by-quarter goal tallies of 6, 8, 8 and 10. Somehow, Batesy, Stephen Bubb and Dukey were considered even more influential and named best afield. Such was the nature of the win, not only did we make the top four, but we jumped from fifth into second and secured the double chance. Fuck me, right?

We entered finals with an incredible amount of lead in our proverbial pencils. The philosophical hard-ons showed as we defeated Uni Blues for the second time in three games in the second semi-final and earnt a spot in the big dance.

We were fixtured to play North Old Boys in the decider at Elsternwick Park after they had defeated Ivanhoe and Uni Blues in their two finals. This game was the reason I had been brought into coach Old Scotch. Phases One and Two were incredibly important, but Phase Three was the reason the Mafia had appointed me at the Flagstaff Hotel. It was the reason John Anderson had turned up to that Reservoir final years earlier. Such was its importance, I'll let Crackers and Browny describe the game.

> Kicking against the wind, the Cardinals trailed by 25 points at quarter-time but by half-time, the deficit had been reduced to seven points. Inaccurate kicking by North Old Boys put them just 17 points ahead at three-quarter time but midway through the last quarter Old Scotch still trailed by 16 points.
>
> Long-time supporters feared a repeat of the heart-breaking 1958 grand final loss. But the Cardinals were not about to cave in! Fighting back desperately with two goals to now trail by just one point, a final goal from Stephen Bubb at the 28-minute mark of the last quarter clinched a five-point victory. North Old Boys then had an opportunity to win the match with

a long-range kick after the siren which just failed to make the distance.

We had done it. We had fucking done it. It took three quarters and another 28 minutes in the fourth, but we achieved what we had set out to do. Batesy was unbelievable in that final with 32 hit-outs in a best-on-ground performance, while Mike Purnell, Jim Marx, Peter Sherwen, John Anderson and Bubb all starred.

Sitting fifth going into the last round of the home and away season, we were A Grade champions one month later. While I had finally accomplished the success I yearned for, I was just as happy for Scotch. They took a punt on a hard-lined Port Melbourne bloke from Reservoir – I bet they never expected to say that - and it came off for both of us. Sitting in the clubrooms after the match, Leigh McGregor sat alongside me.

Laurie, the Old Boys can't explain how delighted we are with what you've done for our club. It's simply amazing.

I'm glad Leigh, but it's my club too, mate.

OLD SCOTCH COLLEGIANS A GRADE PREMIERS (1978)

If the 1978 premiership was the pinnacle of Amateur football, 1979 was the total and complete opposite. With Batesy and Dukey experiencing season-ending injuries and several premiership players content with one flag, we finished last on the ladder with a 4-14 record. Back to B Grade. Many supporters called it a premiership hangover. I called it as I saw in the club newsletter.

> The reasons are very clear to everyone. There were many great players who were either injured or by selfish design, decided that the job we started four years ago was finished and they had fulfilled their commitment to the club. They had, in fact, only satisfied their own selfish attitude, hence our setback.
>
> Scotchies, starting from this very instant, players, club members, supporters with tongue between teeth, with deep desire and enthusiasm, with strength of character and total commitment, let us fight back to the top, let us combine unity and strength, let us have no self-pity or excuses, our rewards will come.

As someone who strives for repeated success, relegation was a tough pill to swallow one year after breaking through for that A Grade flag. I was frustrated with the perceived lack of commitment early in the season. By Round 3, it all boiled over.

It had been three years since an altercation took place between University Blues and Batesy while he was still playing for Reservoir. I had just moved to Scotch at the time, but it was well-known that the incident was ugly. By Round 3 in 1979, the Blues had not forgotten about the altercation and one of their players, Peter Karvelis, started scrapping with Batesy in the Blues' forward line. It was clearly retribution. Karvelis continued his tirade against Batesy at three-quarter time and, in doing so, found himself far too close to our huddle. As he jogged past our group with his shit-eating grin and incessant slurs, he made a grave error in judgement and walked next to me. Before I knew it, he was flat on his back. An Aghan special to the jaw. Such was the speed and precision of the left hook, one could have been forgiven for thinking he fainted. To be perfectly honest, I didn't even see the punch myself. One of the officiating goal umpires came streaming towards me and reported me for striking. For fuck's sake. I was suspended for three weeks, and the club was fined $300.

Karvelis and the Blues were found guilty of breaching the amateur status with a false registration form one year later and subsequently relegated to B Section for the 1981 season. While I may have copped a suspension and cost the club a little bit of money, it was well worth it.

The new decade brought about a new goal as we tried to earn promotion back to A Grade. On the back of standout seasons from Tom Mason, Paul Meadows, and Peter Sherwen, we were successful in gaining promotion but fell short of another premiership with a two-point loss to Old Xaverians. We didn't go home empty handed though as the reserves thumped Old Xavs by 57 points earlier in the day. It was my first and only reserves premiership at Scotch and almost made up for the seniors' loss. In fact, that reserves flag was the last crumb of success I would ever taste at the club.

My time at Old Scotch was ending. I approached the 1981 season with the same vigour and expectation as '78, but I was missing the talent. We finished seventh that season, and I knew it was the end. The end of an era. Brian Gibbs approached me and asked for my thoughts on the appointment of Pete Sherwen as senior coach. For various reasons, I agreed and stood down.

1978 OSFC LIFE MEMBERS & PART OF THE SCOTCH MAFIA

I made a brief return to the club when I accepted the role of Under 19s coach in 1988 while Jason was playing and took the reins of the seniors once more in 1990. By that time, the culture of the club had changed. I didn't agree with the direction it was heading so I didn't stay.

That 1978 senior premiership remains the most recent in the club's history. Despite spending a record 35 straight years in A Grade from 1981, they haven't been able to replicate the success of that incredible '78 team.

I spent seven years of my life coaching the seniors and reserves at Old Scotch for three premierships. From four players at a BBQ to the club's first A Grade premiership in 44 years, the ride was incredible. I was lucky enough to receive life membership in 1988 and I was named as coach in the Old Scotch Team of the 20th Century in 2000. Accolades I never set out to achieve but hold dearly to this day.

People often ask me about the differences between coaching Reservoir OB and Old Scotch. There weren't many. The main difference was the way Scotch supporters reacted to me telling Ivanhoe's Jimmy Robertson that if he calls us public school poofs once more, I'll *'fucking knock you right out mate'*. Reservoir wouldn't have battered an eyelid. Ultimately, Reservoir wanted to win. Old Scotch wanted to win. And during my tenure at both clubs, we won. And we were grinning.

VALE JOHN ANDERSON

Never in my life have I seen a man so committed to his football club. Six-time best and fairest winner, seven seasons as captain of the club, committeeman, the list goes on. Ando wanted nothing but success for the Old Scotch Collegians FC.

The year he died we were having lunch in Camberwell. Our footy club was struggling, and he wanted to help.

> *Mate, let's go back and work in the administration of the club. We can raise money and help with player programs, injured players and young men looking for work.'*

That's the type of bloke he was.

The news of his death in Mykonos was gut wrenching. I will always think of you, mate. Everything you gave me and the Old Scotch FC.

Brian Gibbs, Geoff McCracken, Leigh McGregor - brilliant men who formed a strong administration.

To my close mates - Simon Tallent, Peter Sherwen, Tim Cox, Tom Mason, Fergus Kiel, Dave Bowden, and Laird Gordon - thank you for the friendship over many years.

To all who helped us achieve over the years, my best wishes.

FOOTY THE GREAT LEVELLER

JOHN ANDERSON: A GREAT MAN

10

THE BIG V

'Don't let the Big V down'
GREG CHAMPION, AUSTRALIAN MUSICIAN.

MOST PEOPLE WOULD AGREE the pinnacle of coaching success is winning premierships. And throughout my VAFA career, I was lucky enough to win nine. Outside of winning flags and pouring VB long necks over your head while listening to Khe Sanh, however, the height of success was being appointed state coach.

At the end of the 1973 season, I was invited to Elsternwick Park to discuss the vacant state coach position with the VAFA Mafia: Jack Fullerton, John Dillon, Noel Rundle, Manson Russel, Alf Keam and John Miles.

Unlike today where coaches are selected when they are no longer directly involved with a club, it was standard practice to reward success with the honour of being the Victorian coach. Following Reservoir's rise from E Section through to B Section (and soon-to-be A), I was at the front of the queue.

The VAFA had scheduled matches against South Australia

and Tasmania the following year and before the interview commenced, Manson inundated me with the history of the of the Big V and the rivalry between the states. Of particular emphasis was the contest between Victoria and South Australia. Or more the fact the Vics had lost their past two and four of their previous five clashes. The upcoming match was fixtured in Norwood, and we hadn't won there since 1966.

Of the 85 representative matches the VAFA had played since 1925, we'd lost just 11 times – and every one of those losses came against the Croweaters. Of course, I had to ask why.

Because they're bloody cheats.

I really should've opened the chapter with that beauty. Jack Fullerton was never one to mince his words. He explained that the South Australian Amateur Football League (SAAFL) team was often stacked with former SANFL players. It would have been the same as the VAFA loading its side with ex-VFL. It wasn't exactly in the rules but never strictly enforced.

The rivalry between the two amateur associations started in 1925. The MAFA (Metropolitan Amateur Football Association as the Vics were known) hosted the SAAFL at the MCG and ran out comprehensive winners, 22.22 (154) to 8.10 (58). The Sporting Globe described the Croweaters' disposal as slow and inaccurate, adding they played as individuals and '*overindulged in foolish handball*'. Nearly 100 years later and one could argue that's still a problem with the game. After slamming the SAAFL's performance in the first-ever interstate match between the teams, the Sporting Globe summarised the entire weekend as follows:

> The Amateurs of both states are to be complimented on their fearless launching of an enterprise that is going

> to improve the standard of the Australian game, and incidentally improve their own status'. – The Sporting Globe (1925).

After that inaugural match, the Vics and South Australians played the first eight interstate matches against one another on a rotation between Melbourne and Adelaide. The Victorians played matches against Tasmania, NSW, Western Australia, Canberra and the VFL/VFA, but the rivalry with the South Australians remained the most important. By the time I was appointed coach at the end of 1973, the two sides had faced each other 41 times and we had won 30 of them. So, to have lost four of their last five with that sort of dominant record, things were currently pretty grim. Jack had his way of describing it.

It's fucked.

One week later, I received a letter from Jack notifying me of the appointment. Despite having limited knowledge of the representative program before that interview, I wanted the role more than anything when I left. It was a reward for my effort and success at club level. It was recognition for my service to the competition. And it was a chance to get one back against those fuckers across the border.

We met again in early May and the Big V committee asked for my opinion of the makeup of the team. It had been several months since my appointment, so I had plenty of time to consider my approach and the theme of leadership I wanted to implement.

I want captains. I want A and B grade captains.

Not only are club captains generally the best players, but they understand the notion of extreme effort as well as anyone and they can play under pressure. Given we had lost four of the past five against the Croweaters, there was serious fucking pressure on the outcome of this upcoming game.

The squad we assembled was outstanding. Using the captaincy formula where possible, we selected champion Amateur players like Bruce Bourne (Ormond), John Anderson (Old Scotch), Greg Tootell (Caulfield Grammarians) and Shane Maguire (North Old Boys).

And then, of course, I had some of my Reservoir boys: Danny Barclay, Terry Archer, and Kevin Grose. I knew I could rely on those three to give me everything. The trio performed well at Norwood, but it was Grosey who turned the match for us.

With the game in the balance at three-quarter time, Grosey approached me at the huddle and asked that I give him free reign to attack in the final term. That is, no defending at all. With little to lose, I allowed it and watched on as he kicked two crucial goals and lifted our side to an 11-point victory, 18.14 (122) to 17.9 (111). It ended a three-year winless run against the Croweaters. To do it in front of their crowd was the cherry on top of a fucking delicious Big V cake.

As Greg Tootell once said to me, *'it was the best game of amateur football I've ever played in'*. As Jack Fullerton said to me more than once, *'we are kings again'*.

I often reminisce on the quality of that side. Alongside Toots, the Reservoir boys, Bruce Bourne & Ando, we had Andrew Ireland, Shane Maguire, Ross Duke, and Bruce Kefford. Serious players. Looking back, how the hell did it get so close?

After the game, Manson Russel, Noel Rundle, and I attended the All-Australian Amateur team selection dinner with officials from South Australia. Despite the fact I was usually a non-drinker, I decided to let my hair down and indulge in the red and white wine on offer. This, as it turned out, was a mistake. Naturally, I was hammered drunk after two glasses. As I left the room at the end of the night, I failed to make the top of the stairs before redecorating the walls with all of God's grape juice. It was everywhere. If only spewing my guts up was the last of it on that night. After leaving the venue, I flagged down a taxi only for a police car to roll up instead. Those taxi-looking police fuckers. After a good chuckle from both officers, they agreed to drive me back to our motel where my embarrassment lasted a lot longer than it should have thanks to the ongoing sledging from Manson and Noel.

BIG V TEAM VS SOUTH AUSTRALIA (1974)

1974 was a successful year for me and the Big V with the other game we played against Tasmania FL resulting in a 35-point victory at Abbotsfield Park in Hobart. I was two from two but, after accepting a role as senior coach at Yarraville the following year, it would be another nine years until I regained the Big V reins.

Upon my return to the position of state coach in 1983, the Big V were once again fixtured to play two games: South Australia and the VFA. Ever since we broke the drought against the Croweaters in '74, the Vics had proceeded to win seven of the next eight games between the two sides, so our 38-point victory that year was expected. It was nice to return to the helm in triumphant fashion, but I knew we had bigger fish to fry.

It was the game against the VFA that had pundits – me included – nervous. Their list was as strong as I'd seen in my short tenure. Former South Melbourne wingman2, Gary Brice, was coaching their squad, while recently retired Collingwood captain, Ray Shaw, was the VFA's skipper. Brice was one thing, but Shaw was another kettle of fish altogether. He could have still been playing league footy if not for his fallout with Collingwood officialdom three years earlier.

In the lead-up to the game, I appeared on Channel 7's World of Sport with Bobby Davis, who asked me point blank how we could possibly win. I explained the Amateur way of life and made it very clear that our players were just as talented as the VFA's. But with lawyers and doctors coming out of our arse, we were also a hell of a lot smarter and had a lot less time to train. We did have six ex-VFL players on our team, but it was nothing like the VFA.

Despite significantly less league talent than our opponents, our team was strong. John Jones and Brian Bourke led as captain and vice-captain, while Chris Stone, Mick Deveson, Billy Nettlefold, Mick Greene, and Shane Murphy were just a fraction of our overall talent.

The match was won and lost with the performance of Billy Nettlefold. Prior to the game, I worded him up about my plans to have him tag Shaw. It was clearly the toughest job on the ground. But after 100 games of league footy with Richmond, North Melbourne, and Melbourne, I had faith in him. I can't exactly remember Billy's response to the news, only that it was a mixture of *'whatever you want, coach'* and *'for fuck's sake!'* I'm sure I referenced Greg Champion's song title more than once while selling Billy on the role.

As it turned out, the decision was a masterstroke. Billy followed Shaw like his shadow, completely curtailing his influence and shutting him out of the game. He tagged him so closely I wouldn't have been surprised if he offered to shake it for him after his half-time piss.

Chris Stone starred through the midfield, while our two young ruckmen, Laurie Stretton and Johnny Twomby, gave us first use all day. 11 points was the margin, 18.16.124 – 16.17.113. It was an incredible team effort and a proud day for the VAFA. A proud day for the Big V.

Of the seven times I was appointed state coach, we suffered just one loss. But fuck me that one loss hurt. I had built a 5-0 win/loss record up until that point, but we were absolutely dismantled by the VFA when we met at Elsternwick Park in 1984. Without beating around the bush, we lost by 51 points, 14.11 (95) to 22.14 (146). 25 scoring shots to 36. Shithouse. More than the score line, the loss stung because of the attitude of the players. I selected in-form players from throughout the top section – as opposed to the captaincy theme implemented from a decade earlier – and they let me down with their attitudes and lack of application. The pride in wearing the jumper was evident in too few. They had let me and the Association down.

My coaching record was no longer perfect. While I can live with that, it's safe to say I couldn't live with another performance like that, so I swung the axe ahead of the next game like

FOOTY THE GREAT LEVELLER

it was the Battle of Troy. And it was those changes that allowed me to leave the state coaching position on a magnificent high.

> AB: "Laurie, how's the boys' attitude in the past 24 hours?"
>
> LA: "We've been together most of the time and training yesterday was brisk and short and I think they're going to acquit themselves very well"
>
> AB: "Quite a few ex-VFL players in your line-up?"
>
> LA: "Yes, we have Chris Stone, Nick Wilton, Nick Burne, Steve Curtain – all pretty polished sort of players. Didn't reach the highlights of league football but good enough to come back and play in representative sides."
>
> AB: "Laurie, you've been coaching these types of sides some 16 years now and how do you compare this particular line-up?"
>
> LA: "I think we've got a better running side than we've ever had, and I came up last year and watched the Australian Amateurs fail against the Country who really deserved their win, they were the better side by far all day. And I think we've got the side to match them today."
>
> AB: "(A) running side most important here on the Queen Elizabeth Oval?"
>
> LA: "Very important. I believe that's where we failed last year, and we've certainly countered that this year."
>
> AB: "Players in the Victorian Country side that you're obviously going to have to keep an eye on?"
>
> LA: "Oh naturally David Code. He is a former Amateur player. Stephen Wells, another former Amateur

player. Probably the two league boys and I believe the young boy that's playing I think it's Comby is it full-forward and naturally Mal Scott – I believe he'll have to be countered. But we're not really worrying about our opposition so much as worrying about our own possession."

AB: "The boys getting together in Bendigo in the last 24 hours, is it good for sides to get away and have they had the right preparation now do you think?"

LA: "Yes, there's no excuses. We've had probably the best preparation of any side and you must realise that a lot of our guys have been together for about 12 weeks now training for the VFA game and the South Australian Amateurs. So, we've had the nucleus there most of the time."

AB: "Alright well good luck this afternoon."

LA: "Thank you Alan, thank you very much."

1984 Pre-game Interview with Alan Besley (VCFL VS VAFA)

After being embarrassed by the VFA less than a month earlier, we made 15 changes for our clash against John Northey's VCFL side in Bendigo. Only Andrew Smyth, Mick Deveson, Nick Burne, Rohan Brown, and Steve Curtain were recalled. John Jones was replaced as captain by Browny, and I added a fleet of smalls, including Frank Gleeson, Ricky Demarte, Dominic Simonetti and Lou Balcombe. High quality smalls tasked with nipping around the feet of Brown, Curtain, Michael Yeo, and Alan Naylor. It was a far more balanced side than the one that lost to the VFA so the confidence I showed in the pre-game interview with Alan was more than justified.

FOOTY THE GREAT LEVELLER

Moments before the game started, a farmer approached me with a wager.

$2000 that the Country will beat your lot, Aghan.

Not today mate. John Dillon's your man.

Normally, I would've accepted it on the spot. I didn't want the stress of the wager and a game we had to win so I put him in touch with John instead. Knowing John as I do, I thought it was safe bet that he'd accept the farmer's offer. I once asked John if he agreed to the wager, but he refused to answer. I must say, the free slabs of beer we got on the way home were fucking fantastic though.

We ended up winning that game by 19 points, 15.10 (100) to 11.15 (81). My representative swansong was a resounding success. Michael Yeo starred alongside every one of the recently added smalls. Ricky Demarte would have collected 35 disposals in a dominant display and should have been awarded best afield. He was sensational. He was quick, he was clean, and he was the main reason we won that day. Our captain, Rohan Brown, was awarded BOG for a strong second half, but Demarte was the star.

The bus trip home with John Dillon's surprisingly generous free beer was one of the great highlights of my time with the Big V. We had just defeated a side who were tipped to destroy us by 10 goals. And we humbled them. We fucking humbled them. John Northey and all his shit talk prior to the match had been humbled. I've never worried about reputations or names. As I learnt from a young age, if they've got two hands, two eyes, two feet, they can be beaten.

BIG V TEAM VS VCFL (1984)

There are many people who act as one's support base during representative programs. Some of my most important were the late Gus Mitchell, my close mate, Dave Urquhart, Dr Brian Costello, Shane Maguire, and Johnny Miles.

The many players who played in these games were the best in the business. They bought into my philosophies, and they executed on six of seven occasions. Thank you for your hard work. It paid off.

Everyone wants to win. Winning in the Big V, however, is far more important than any club game. We are not just representing ourselves in those matches, but the entire Association. They've put their faith in us, so for Christ's sake, don't let them down. Don't let the Big V down.

FOOTY THE GREAT LEVELLER

> 1122 Burke Rd,
> Nth Balwyn. 3104.
> 11·7·74
>
> Dear Laurie,
>   I didn't have a good chance at the airport to thank you properly for all you've done for me + my football. I knew I was a long shot as regards selection for the S.A. side + I am really grateful for your faith in me. Thankyou also for taking me for the Australian side + the Taroy side both of those trips were really great experiences. I've gained alot out of meeting you + being coached by you + its you I've got to thank for the big V which means so much to me. Best of luck for the rest of the season + I'll see you again for sure.
>
>   Bruce Kefford.

BRUCE KEFFORD'S LETTER TO LAURIE (9174)

> 9/1 Cotham Rd,
> Kew Vic 3101
> 28/8/82.
>
> Laurie,
>   Nice to read that story about you in the Herald — Congratulations on your magnificent efforts during the seventies and early eighties. What a pity I couldn't talk the Collingwood Committee into appointing or approaching you in 1975 — anyway their loss was the Amateurs good fortune. I hope you continue to enjoy your life in sport for many people will look back in later life and be grateful for the smaterie you gave them.
>   Regards
>   Bill Twomey.

BILL TWOMEY'S LETTER TO LAURIE (1982)

11
OLD MELBURNIANS, BULLEEN TEMPLESTOWE & AQUINAS
(1982 & 1983) (1985) (2000 & PART 2001)

'If what you did yesterday seems big, you haven't done anything today.

LOU HOLTZ, FORMER NOTRE DAME MEN'S FOOTBALL COACH.

HAVING COMPLETED COACHING STINTS at both Reservoir and Old Scotch, I was done. Finished. I had given everything I had to those two VAFA clubs. We'd won premierships, reached A Grade and I had only punched a handful of blokes. Wins all around.

I was enjoying my newfound freedom shortly after leaving Old Scotch when my phone rang. As you've probably noticed throughout this book, every time my phone rings, it's usually accompanied by an offer of some sort. This was no different.

Laurie, it's Rohan Brown and Ian Cordner from Old Melburnians.

Boys, I've not even had time to breathe.

Just hear us out. We'll come to your office.

Bloody hell, OK.

When the pair of Old Melburnians champions arrived in my East Brunswick office, I was adamant that I was never going to coach again. Absolutely adamant. Not happening. Well, for the first two hours it wasn't happening. After that, however, they were basically selling ice to Eskimo Aghan. At the very least, I was questioning my decision. Maybe it was too early to retire from coaching? I mean, I had nothing else to do. Plenty of time on my hands. What's the worst thing that could happen? These two will be named Big V Legends at the end of their careers, let alone their teammates back in the sheds. It's a high-quality list. Fuck it, I'm going around again. As Big Lou from Notre Dame said, if what I'd achieved at Reservoir and the Cardinals was big, I hadn't done anything today.

The only real consideration I had to weigh up was making the move from Scotch to Melbourne Grammar. Two private school rivals; one of which I'd taken to the top of the tree. Would the two camps be any different? While I'm sure Scotchies and Grammar boys will have many reasons why they're better than the other, I couldn't see a difference. Yes, they were likely all well off financially, but they also all wanted to win. All the time. I fucking loved that.

I met with Rohan, Ian, and Gary Austin to work out the terms of the arrangement. As always, I needed to have control of both the seniors and reserves. Sole coach of the club. It had worked at my previous two amateur clubs, and I wasn't about to mess with a winning formula. Thankfully, neither were they.

Overseeing both sides was of the utmost importance to me throughout my career. It stemmed from my time at Reservoir when I noticed a disconnect between the seniors and reserves players. Why would we have a separation of teams? It didn't make sense to me. Coaching both meant we were all heading in the same direction. Same game plan. Same instructions. One out, one in. It wasn't exactly a headscratcher.

It also put an end to any favouritism, with every player getting a game based purely on merit. There were always dickheads and shit stirrers who had the ability to cause division by refusing to allow their players to be picked by the higher-ranked team. That was never going to fly with me. It allowed me to build connections with not just every player at the club, but the assistant coaches, the officials, and the volunteers. Strong relationships are, without question, the most important component of any football club and I think we did better than anyone.

Ahead of the 1982 season, Old Melburnians were playing and training at Fawkner Park in South Yarra. This is an important detail because that club has had more homes than an adolescent Laurie Aghan. And some of them would have given Camp

Pell a run for its money regarding the aesthetics and playing surface. But Fawkner Park was fantastic.

Having finished in the middle of B Grade in 1981, OMs were another proud school-based team hellbent on returning to the top tier of VAFA football. Barry Morphet, a star player and loyal Old Melburnian, approached me at training during pre-season and explained how much the players needed discipline. They had the talent, but they hadn't yet harnessed it. He was adamant that if I could instill a disciplined approach with these teams, they would be incredibly successful.

Discipline came easily. We worked hard. Fucking hard. The boys responded well, and we were absolutely humming heading into Round 1. There were a few hiccups along the way, and I'll always remember the time a young Rick Pisarski showcased a level of behaviour I didn't think quite hit the 'disciplined' mark.

If you're not going to listen to me Rick,
you can piss off mate.

What did you just say to me?

Colour me shocked, Rick didn't appreciate the way I spoke to him, and we almost came to blows. It wouldn't have been the first physical altercation over my training methods, but it could've been my last. A young Rick was an imposing figure and there's no doubt he could've held his own. I'm not sure who benefited more from the incident being broken up, but Rick later apologised for his part in the exchange. I was happy he did because he became a fine talent and the backbone of the club for many years.

We had several talented players on the list, but one who stood out more than most was school-aged star, Ian McMullin.

A noted half-forward with a superb head of hair, Ian's silky skills and knack for finding the goals would have put the lead in the proverbial pencil of any amateur coach and I was no exception.

He was recruited to Collingwood two years later (1984) and displayed his elite skillset with eight goals in his first four games. With 49 matches to his name across nine seasons at the Pies and Essendon, I can't help but think he was underutilised at the elite level. Still, he was an important piece to my puzzle in '82 and a decorated Old Melburnian for many years.

I was incredibly lucky to coach Ian during that 1982 season, as I was too with Rohan Brown (captain), Ian Cordner, Edward Cordner, Rick Pisarski, Andrew Witts, and Barry Morphet. Before diving into the exploits of our premiership campaign, it would be remiss of me not to touch on the impact the Cordner boys and their family had on our season, the club, and the Association more broadly.

The Cordners are considered the 'first family' of amateur football, with four generations of involvement. According to *For the Love of the Game 1892-1992,* it was not just footballing success that earned the Cordner family their unique status, but the spirit in which they played the game. As Don Cordner once said:

> I thoroughly enjoyed my playing association with football but the sport, especially at AFL level, occupies a position of prominence and influence in Melbourne out of all possible proportion to its true value and its contribution to society. The amount of time, expense, publicity and general hoo-hah squandered on League football is a measure of our sense of values and priorities, and we as citizens should be concerned about it.

The family were incredible proponents of amateurism and the VAFA – or MAFA for those dating back far enough – and I was lucky enough to have two of them running around in the navy blue. Ian had already tasted success at University Blacks eight years earlier, while Edward was himself an interstate amateur.

We had an incredible season in '82 and finished in the top two. After losing the second semi-final to Ivanhoe by 15 points – the third time we'd lost to them that season – we hit back with a comprehensive 43-point victory over Kew. Our grand final spot had been booked. Thankfully, the hat-trick of losses we experienced at the hands of Ivanhoe through the year ended on grand final day. We were sensational, running out winners, 18.7.115 – 15.12.102.

In one season, we were back in A Grade. Richard Cameron was particularly influential throughout the finals series, backing up from his 85 goals throughout the home and away season with another 18 in September. He wasn't the only one to star for us that year, with Ian Cordner kicking 52 and Rohan Brown finishing equal-second in the B Grade best & fairest. Looking back now, the success we experienced should come as no surprise given six of our premiership players were named in the OMFC Team of the Century: R. Pisarski, B.A. Morphet, R.I. Cordner (VC), I.C. McMullin, R.B. Brown, and A.E. Witts (DVC).

It was equally important that we made the reserves grand final in the same season. Unfortunately, we went down to Bulleen Templestowe after I had to leave for the seniors with the game in the balance at three-quarter time. It was one of the very few regrets I had coaching both sides because we should have gone back to A Grade with two flags in tow. It certainly didn't stop the celebrations in the party house on Punt Road – always well-frequented and as loose as any I've ever seen. Fuck me, those Melbourne Grammar boys knew how to turn one on.

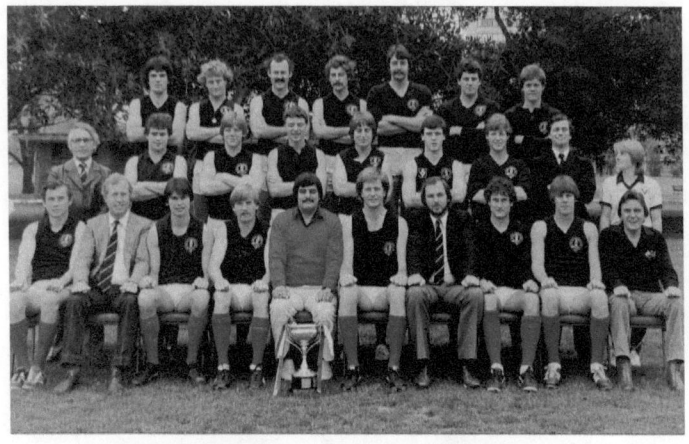

OLD MELBURNIANS SENIOR B GRADE PREMIERS (1982)

The following year derived a great sense of disappointment, with 13 players from our premiership team moving on. 13 fucking players. For obvious reasons, we couldn't replace that number of personnel in one off-season and having re-entered A Grade, we struggled accordingly. It felt as though we hadn't even kicked a pill as an A Grade side before dropping straight back down. At the time, I was frustrated and emotional, and called it a wasted year. That was a stupid comment from a silly old bastard. I made exceptional friends during my time at OMs, with Dave Urquhart, Ross Middleton, and Barry Morphet taking the cake. On and off the field, those three backed me 100%. And for that, I'll be forever grateful.

After one arbitrary season of coaching Bulleen Templestowe's seniors and reserves in 1985, I moved around for one-season stints at Templestowe (1986), Old Scotch Under 19s (1988), Old Scotch again (1990) and North Ringwood (1991). These hit and run missions eventually had to end, and it was at the conclusion of that season with North Ringwood that I decided to officially hang up the clipboard. I was cooked and I needed a break. That break, well it lasted the best part of eight years.

Ahead of the 2000 VAFA season, I received a phone call from my son's work colleague, Howie Field, gauging my interest in coaching Aquinas OCFC. Much like Reservoir when I first arrived, Aquinas were in a lowly section but had the will to rise. Howie explained as succinctly as one could.

> *Mate, we've got no money to offer you, but we've got a great group of young blokes.*
>
> *I've been out of the game for eight years.*
>
> *It's Division 1 mate, you'll be fine.*
>
> *Alright, I want both seniors and reserves, and Freddy Tuininga is helping out.*

While the conversation may have been slightly longer than four lines, you get the point. I had one last shot at creating another story akin to Reservoir's and I was going to attempt it at Aquinas. The mighty Bloods. A club that had won an E East Section flag just four years earlier but had seemingly stalled since. Pre-season was fantastic, the players had enormous upside, a bloke called Andy Cultrera was running around and the signs of another fairytale Reservoir story were starting to come together.

After finishing third in the regular season and earning a finals berth, history repeated somewhat when three key players broke curfew and had an all-nighter. Or a bender. Either way, it was a shitshow. We ended up getting beaten the following day and finished the year in fourth spot. The players involved apologised for their behaviour, but it was too late. Their chance of immediate success had gone begging. It would take another 17 years before the Bloods experienced premiership glory again.

While I was disappointed with how it finished, I gave it my all. I had already garnered great success at Reservoir, Scotch and Old Melburnians, but failed to crack the code at Aquinas. That's life. I couldn't rest on my laurels. It wasn't in me to do that. If what I did yesterday seemed big, I hadn't done anything today.

LAURIE'S TOP 30 VAFA PLAYERS

1. Ross Duke (Old Paradians, Old Scotch)
2. Michael Bates (Reservoir OB, Old Scotch)
3. John Anderson (Old Scotch)
4. Kevin Grose (Reservoir OB)
5. Danny McGaw (Reservoir OB)
6. Ian McMullin (Old Melburnians)
7. Rohan Brown (Old Melburnians)
8. Chris Stone (Old Caulfield)
9. Ian Cordner (Uni Blacks, Old Melburnians)
10. Bruce Bourne (Ormond)
11. Peter Murnane (De La Salle)
12. Andrew Ireland (Ivanhoe)
13. Peter Sherwen (Old Scotch)
14. John Jones (Marcellin)
15. Mick Jennings (Uni Blues)
16. Andrew Smythe (Bulleen Templestowe)
17. Peter Brown (Old Scotch)
18. Mike Yeo (Uni Blues)
19. Peter Gittos (Ivanhoe)
20. Mick Deveson (De La Salle)

21. Paul Considine (North Old Boys)
22. Nick Burne (Old Xaverians)
23. Nick Wilton (Old Xaverians)
24. Bernie Cooper (Marcellin)
25. Mark Brody (St Kevin's OB)
26. Billy Nettlefod (St Kevin's OB)
27. Rick Pisarski (Old Melburnians)
28. Phil Cleary (Coburg)
29. Simon Tallent (Old Scotch)
30. Ray Shepherd (Reservoir OB, Ivanhoe)

12

THE DEMISE OF AUSTRALIAN RULES

'Pigs arse.'

JOHN ELLIOT, FORMER CARLTON FC PRESIDENT.

FOR A MOMENT, PLEASE allow me to indulge. Allow me to reminisce about the 'good old days' and how I've seen them change over time. Because they have. I'm not sure it's been for the betterment of the game. In fact, I'm sure it hasn't.

Football was created to be a spectacle. High marks, long kicks and brutal physical contact were the key pillars to the greatest game on earth.

It was a game often of unpredictability, from the bounce of the ball to the swirliness of the wind or the condition of the playing surface. It didn't matter if it was played in extremely muddy conditions or a perfect winter's day, goals were kicked, and scores were often high.

There were five dangerous positions on the ground: full back, centre-half back, centre, centre-half forward and full forward. The idea was to create quick ball movement from one end to the other in a bid to score.

At this stage of the book, you can probably safely assume I'm a big fan of community footy. That's where the game is at its purest and its best.

Teams from all walks of life formed competitions. These teams were made up of a senior coach, an assistant, and a playing group. Overseeing the whole club was an honorary committee. The secretary was the most important role on the committee – much like the engine room through the midfield, it's their job to keep the game moving. Players worked full-time, trained 2-3 times a week and paid their club minor costs to assist with insurance, affiliation fees and potentially some ground maintenance. Even some coaches did it for the love of the game. You're reading the story of one who rarely got paid. I never gave a shit about the money. And it worked. No financial incentive made it a pure brand of the game we all love.

Community clubs were largely made up of three teams: seniors, reserves and Under 19s. The underage teams were often administered by volunteer parents, most of whom would navigate between football in the winter and cricket in the summer.

The major costs associated with football at that level were jumpers, medical supplies, and sporting equipment. Small sponsors, families, and the weekly chook raffle often covered these costs, and prizes were donated.

Ultimately, clubs and competitions remained healthy because of small costs and great community involvement. This ensured an even playing field for all clubs as they were all operating under similar financial constraints. Football was booming. It was bloody great.

Over time, however, success became more important. Winning became everything. Clubs decided to pay players for their services. I will always remember the day Hassa Mann told me he received 25 quid to play in a grand final. I couldn't believe it. Not because he didn't deserve it – fuck knows he deserved it – but because it just wasn't the done thing.

This evolved into coaches receiving payments and even club administrators. Expenses exploded and football, as we knew it, became a business. This required sponsors with deep pockets. It required financial backers. It required funneling more and more power into less and less people. Can you see where I'm going with this?

The introduction of money created problems for players and clubs alike. The game started to suffer as teams constantly attempted to outdo each other with financial incentives aimed at the most talented players. Loyalty to the club and to the jumper waned and the game itself started to lose support. Financial inequality grew as a lot of clubs simply couldn't compete with the 'mafia' organisations. Ultimately, this resulted in clubs folding and entire competitions ceasing to exist.

Despite being ineligible to pay players in the Amateurs, the pinch of increased costs was still felt across the board. Affiliation fees, ground maintenance, every conceivable financial aspect of running a football club increased. It took its toll. Just look at my Reservoir Old Boys. Once a powerhouse of the competition, it was forced to disband only a few years after reaching the heights of A Grade football.

But what does the future hold?

Honestly, who knows? What we do know is that many community football clubs are in serious financial trouble. The effects of COVID-19 are still being felt with a high percentage of players not returning to the game, sponsors pulling out due to their own financial difficulties and with the increased cost of living. Some clubs have been forced to merge. Some have already disbanded. Some are on the verge of folding altogether. It's devastating.

The salaries for coaches, administrators and players are still high and it's killing the local game. If something doesn't change soon, we will go the way of American football or basketball where it's simply too expensive to run.

How can clubs support a senior coach, line coaches and paid administration? The truth is that not all can. Let's not over-exaggerate the game. Stick to what works and keep more teams on the park.

Turning my attention to the modern game, it is a terrible mess. My honest and simple thought is that the game is in a bad place. There are too many rule changes and the whole game has basically been programmed for robots. The basic fundamentals have disappeared and the game as we knew it has changed forever.

It's a game of keepings off. The handball is overused and the dash and dare that made footy a much-watch spectacle has been lost because of it.

I feel sorry for modern-day coaches. They're expected to coach their players to within an inch of a robotic game plan for every second of the game. Players are no longer allowed to think for themselves, take the game on and use their God-given talent to excite the crowd. Where are the long goals? Or the screamers? Or the unrelenting attack on the ball? Where's the loyalty to clubs?

It's not the same and it's just not as good.

As you know by now, I have an opinion and I'm not afraid to share it. I will add, however, that many players, coaches, and officials from yesteryear agree the game has been messed around with far too much.

I recently watched North Melbourne and Geelong

accumulate more than 600 possessions between them. Geelong won the game with less than 10 goals. Yep, 600 disposals and the winning team couldn't even kick 10 bloody goals. The high marks, long kicks and brutal physical contact were non-existent.

Is that a better game than what we produced in the past? Pigs arse it is.

13

THE FAMILY

> 'There is no such thing as a self-made man. You will reach your goals only with the help of others.'
>
> **GEORGE SHINN, FORMER OWNER OF THE CHARLOTTE HORNETS.**

HE'S NOT WRONG.

There have been many special people in my life whose profound impact has always helped me on my own journey. But no one comes close to my wife, Lorna May Barker.

Through years of successes, hardships, motherhood, grandparenthood, and everything in between, this amazing girl has been the shining beacon of my life.

When we first met, I was a bum. A complete no-hoper. No money, one pair of undies, old reefer jacked trousers with torn pockets and certainly no future. This gracious young woman looked past the obvious case of financial insecurity and thought *'I can do something with this bloke'*. Her love, her decent attitude, her special way of whipping me into shape was unique and it was effective. I must have frustrated every fibre of her being with my behaviour at times, but she never complained. Well, not to my face.

Lorna is very much like her parents, Jean and George. They were simple people who always gave you a sense of security. Don't worry, Jeanie could be tough – and trust me, Lorna can be very tough – but in all the time I knew her and George, I never heard them argue. Not once.

Lorna and I have two magnificent children, Kimberly Nicole and Jason Lawrence, both of whom have always been family oriented. Our grandchildren: Lily May, Jake Thomas, Mia Anne, and Jordan Lawrence. They are the four apples of our eyes. Of course, none of this would have been possible without our son-in-law Justin and former daughter-in-law, Sally. Both of whom we love immensely. Unfortunately, Jason and Sally were unable to go the distance. Again, that's life. But the kids were superb throughout the separation. It must be the Aghan blood.

OK, let's rewind for a moment.

Lorna and I lived in many places until we moved to Chelsea Heights, Donvale and finally to our family home in Lincoln Park, Croydon. We certainly had our fair share of challenges in the early days, but Jean and George would often travel to Donvale and deliver bags full of groceries. They knew we were struggling financially and did their utmost to keep us afloat.

Fortune and a bit of luck came our way, so we sold Donvale and moved into Lincoln Park. No mortgage, no stressful overheads, life was good. With my position as senior coach at Old Scotch, I was able to gain Jason admission to the school with the generous assistance of **Leigh McGregor and Brian Steele**. It's something I've never forgotten and will forever be indebted to them for.

More luck came our way when I spent $15 on a few TattsLotto tickets and won a healthy amount of the green stuff. Finally, we had some breathing room.

There were so many people who played a role in my life, so please let me indulge as I acknowledge some of them. After all, this is my book and if you haven't realised yet, I'm doing it my way.

THE MANSONS

Dan and Stella Manson and Dan Jr stepped in when I was down and out. Stella was like a mother to me, she was tough – yes, there's a theme here – but she fed me and occasionally even gave me a bed to sleep in.

THE BOGDANOFFS

Annie, Tony, and their young Tony Jr also gave me support when needed. Food and shelter. God knows I needed it.

THE KERRS

During my saddest and most depressing days living in the slums without money, a job, or much hope at all, it was Brian 'Moey' Kerr and his wife Florence who showed me a new way of life. Moey was like an older brother to me. He got me a job and showed me that life was only worth living if you were having fun. When Moey passed, I couldn't believe it. He was meant to live forever. Florence has also passed, and I was fortunate to deliver the eulogy at both services. I will never forget them.

REGGIE AND MARGARET SMYTHE

This bloke was a genuine handful and always lived life to the fullest. We played footy together and we played life together. When we knocked about and got in trouble – more often than I'll ever admit in this book - he would never leave you to your own devices and would always try and bail you out of situations. He would ring and we would talk for hours and hours, laughing and giggling like schoolgirls as we re-lived the good old times. Mates for over 60 years, this bloke always has your back.

JOHN AND WIN MAY

Mayzie – this man is a saint and I love him dearly. He is still one of my closest mates and to this day we still share holidays together, whether it be in Australia or overseas. Through cancer and blood clot scares, Mayzie has always been with me. He is one man you would go to war with.

MARGARET AND FRED TUININGA

Fred was the captain and president of Reservoir Old Boys, and he is the godfather to our son, Jason. He is a fair dinkum, honest family man with strong Christian beliefs who plays by the book. You need these people in your life and he is mine. Another I've gone to battle with over the years and would continue to do so.

BOB AND ANNE RENNIE

Bob is a workmate but, just as importantly, he's a golf mate. We've had many great times together and still do – when I brain him on the back nine.

GLENYS AND HASSA MANN

These two are close family friends. This is obviously despite my early opinion of the man detailed in this book. Remember, the prick? We have been on many overseas holidays together with Mayzie and he is still one of the Friday golf team. He's chairman of our investment group and I still regard his induction into the VFL Hall of Fame as one of my most proud moments. Most importantly, he's family and always will be.

I'd also like to touch on a couple of stars I played alongside throughout my life. **Jimmy Penaluna** was a hot-headed rover (my kind of operator) and a premiership teammate of mine. His loyalty was profound and still is to this day.

And **Sparra**. He was always working for the Port Colts FC; he was a successful coach and enjoyed a lifetime in football.

The Port boys who are still with us meet once a month in Bay Street for a coffee and many, many laughs. Between the 20 of us, the kicks are continually getting longer, the marks are getting higher and there are always more goals than last month. Geez, I love those boys.

No successes I had in my life would have been achieved alone. I've lived a special life with special people. We're a family. In fact, we're a team. A great bloody team.

LAURIE AGHAN AND NICK ARMISTEAD

LAURIE & LORNA

www.ingramcontent.com/pod-product-compliance
Lightning Source LLC
LaVergne TN
LVHW090041080526
838202LV00046B/3916